DOING THEOLOGY, DOING JUSTICE

DOING THEOLOGY, DOING JUSTICE

JERRY FOLK

FORTRESS PRESS
Minneapolis

DOING THEOLOGY, DOING JUSTICE

Scripture quotations unless otherwise noted are from the Revised Standard Version of the Bible, copyright © 1946, 1952, and 1971 by the Division of Christian Education of the National Council of Churches.

Cover design by Carol Evans-Smith
Book design by Publishers' WorkGroup

Library of Congress Cataloging-in-Publication Data

Folk, Jerry L.
    Doing theology, doing justice / Jerry Folk.
      p. cm.
    Includes bibliographical references and index.
    ISBN 0-8006-2426-2 (alk. paper)
    1. Sociology, Christian.   2. Christianity and justice.   3. Peace—
Religious aspects—Christianity.   4. Theology, Doctrinal.
I. Title.
BT738.F64   1991
261.8—dc20   90-45908
                                                     CIP

The paper used in this publication meets the minimum requirements of American National Standard for Information Sciences—Permanence of Paper for Printed Library Materials, ANSI Z329.48–1984. ∞™

Manufactured in the U.S.A.   AF 1–2426

95   94   93   92   91   1   2   3   4   5   6   7   8   9   10

In Memory of
Harold R. Folk (1908–1988)
and
Olive A. Folk (1904–1989)

CONTENTS

Preface   ix

Introduction   1

PART ONE: THE SOCIAL REALITY OF OUR TIME

1. Serpentine Wisdom in an Age of Crisis   7

2. The Dynamics of Underdevelopment   31

3. The Nuclear Threat to Survival   49

PART TWO: THE TRIUNE GOD AND THE
QUEST FOR JUSTICE AND PEACE

4. God and Israel   65

5. Jesus, God and the Kingdom   91

6. The Political Significance of Jesus' Death and Resurrection   117

7. The Paschal Mystery as Revelation of God   127

Notes   143

Annotated Bibliography   169

Indexes
  Subjects and Names   177
  Scripture   181

PREFACE

I have long needed to relate in one meaningful whole both my Christian faith and my concern for a just, peaceful and ecologically sustainable world. For the sake of my own spiritual, intellectual and ethical development, I felt compelled to reflect on and formulate the questions addressed in this book in the hope of moving toward such an integrated vision.

I believe that this book will be helpful to others who love both God and the world and who want to bring these two loves together in a fruitful relationship. If so, it will not be because the book offers answers but because it raises important questions, provokes reflection, and helps readers to nurture and sustain a life style grounded in a religiously coherent vision of justice and peace.

My confidence that this volume will prove useful is bolstered by the process through which it took shape. It grew out of numerous workshops I have conducted and classes I have taught at churches, conferences, colleges, and seminaries throughout the country. People of all ages, all races, and from several countries participated in these events—male and female, clergy and laity. Though I was the teacher or leader, I also was taught by the participants, and I share in these pages what I learned from them as well as from my own study and experience. As a fruit of this process, this book will be helpful not only to individuals seeking to bring their love of God and of the world together, but also, I believe, to college and seminary teachers, pastors, and leaders of adult and youth study groups in parishes.

In many ways, this book belongs to all those who have participated in the dialogue out of which it grew. They are too numerous to name here, but they know who they are and I acknowledge my debt to them.

In this Preface, however, I would like to name a few people whose contributions were crucial. First, I thank my wife, Kathy, whose challenges have kept me honest and far more open than I otherwise would be. Second, I thank my children, Stephanie and Christopher, who help keep me in touch with my humanity and with what the struggle is all about. Special thanks are also due to the executive board of the SHALOM Center, Sioux Falls, South Dakota, for encouraging me in this work and for granting me a sabbatical 1985–1986, without which this book probably would never have been finished. Thanks to the Lutheran School of Theology in Chicago, which gave us housing during my sabbatical and also offered us a warm, welcoming and very cosmopolitan community. Thanks also to Jean Assmus, Lisa Berridge, Scott Holl, and John Burgess, who typed the manuscript, and to Stephanie Egnotovich, the competent and sensitive editor who improved this book in numerous ways. Finally, thanks to my parents, Harold and Olive Folk, who, as far back as I can remember, always encouraged me to explore both Christian faith and God's world.

Oak Park, Illinois   —Jerry Folk

INTRODUCTION

Contemporary social reality and human experience must be in dialogue with a biblically and historically informed Christian faith. Without such dialogue, there can be no meaningful Christian theology or mission in today's world. In this book, I work to bring such dialogue to fruition.

In Part One I examine the social reality of our time, identifying some of its salient features and some of the major challenges with which it confronts the human community. In this discussion, I move beyond the descriptive to the analytical level, beyond a discussion of symptoms to an examination of causes.

In Part Two I consider anew some of the fundamental beliefs of the Christian faith in light of the awareness of our world and ourselves that emerges from Part One. I believe that out of such theological reflection, guided by the Holy Spirit and informed by love for and understanding of this world, can come a vision informed by faith, which is beautiful, pervasive and powerful enough to help humanity out of the potentially fatal morass into which it has wandered. If this is to happen, however, theologians and all religious people must be willing to risk articulating their faith in new ways and drawing new conclusions about its meaning

for contemporary living. This risk requires trust in the power of the
Holy Spirit to reveal the mysteries of faith for life in our age.

HOLISTIC SALVATION

The fundamental theological presupposition that informs this
book is that the salvation that God offers and the church is to
proclaim and realize in this world is holistic. It embraces all dimensions of reality and human experience—body and mind, the conscious and unconscious, matter and spirit, the individual and
society, the political and the religious. This biblical understanding
of salvation acknowledges the interconnectedness of all things and
recognizes that the salvation and fulfillment of each part or person
is achieved only in and with the salvation of the whole. This holistic understanding of salvation is expressed by the fact that the
Hebrew word *shalom*—which means total well-being—is sometimes
translated in the Septuagint by the Greek word for salvation, *sotería*.
Thus, for the Septuagint translators *shalom* as total well-being is a
synonym for salvation.[1]

Christianity's holistic understanding of salvation is reflected in
the major Christian doctrines of creation, incarnation, resurrection
of the body, and sanctification or transfiguration of believers and
the cosmos. It is also reflected in the centrality of the sacraments in
Christian life and worship. God comes to us not through Word
alone, but through Word incarnate in matter. God comes in the
bread and wine of the Eucharist, in the water of Baptism, and in
the flesh and blood of fellow believers who make up the community of faith, the body of Christ. God comes in a special way in
what the theologians of the early church often referred to as the
other "sacrament," the suffering flesh of the least of our brothers
and sisters (Matthew 25). This Christian understanding of God's
coming as consistently incarnational and sacramental led Anglican
Archbishop William Temple to remark that Christianity is the most
materialistic of the world's religions.

If the church takes seriously the holistic character of the salvation it is called to proclaim and sacramentally embody on earth,
it will come into conflict with the principalities and powers of this
world, just as Jesus and the prophets before him did. This should

come as no surprise to Christians because Jesus warned us many times to expect the hostility of the world and not to put our hands to the plough unless we were prepared for it.

But why must this be so? Why does the world close itself off to its own deliverance? Because the deliverance that the church proclaims and embodies in the power of the Spirit is the coming of a *new creation*, a new cosmic and social order radically different from the one over which the principalities and powers of this world preside. Indeed, it turns this old order upside down and is therefore experienced as a threat by all of us who live in the old order and especially by those who preside over it. Those who live in and preside over this world are perhaps willing to accept the idea of God's reign coming sometime—but not here, not now. Yet it is precisely this here-and-nowness that Jesus announces and that the paschal event in which Jesus' life culminated confirms. The life, death and resurrection of Jesus calls the new creation into existence here and now, in the midst of the old. The present power of this new creation is already putting the mighty down from their thrones and exalting the humble, already filling the hungry with good things and sending the rich away empty, already making the first last and the last first. The old is already beginning to pass away, the world is already being turned upside down. It is the presence of this end-time reality here and now that the principalities and powers object to, not the abstract idea of an end of time. Nevertheless, the mission of the church is to live out its belief that the kingdom is already the determining reality among us, despite the old world order. In the face of such hostility from the old order, Christians may sometimes be tempted to become self-righteous or cynical. At such times, we need to remember our own sinfulness and to cry out to God for deliverance from such attitudes, so inconsistent with the life of faith, hope and love to which we are called.

SERPENTINE WISDOM

A second presupposition of this study follows from the first. If the church is called to proclaim and mediate to society a salvation that is holistic, then knowledge of society in its many dimensions is of great importance. Too often, Christians are naïve about society.

There are no doubt many reasons for this naïveté. Whatever its causes, however, such naïveté makes the church's evangelistic task more difficult and its witness less credible.

The prophets and Jesus were not naïve about their societies. They did not look on the surface of things or accept the "official" explanations and justifications. They saw through things and into things. They exposed the underlying, shadowy side of human society and discredited the idolatrous and self-serving myths by which their societies justified themselves. This understanding of his world contributed to Jesus' power and increased the threat posed by him and his movement to the existing social order and its rulers.

Jesus' advice to his followers to understand their society and to penetrate and expose the self-justifying myths by which it lived is the point of one of the most difficult of his parables—the parable of the Unjust Steward (Luke 16:1-19). It is also the point of Jesus' exhortation in Matthew 10:16 to be "wise as serpents." Jesus here advises his followers, whom he is about to send on a mission into the world, to practice the same serpentine wisdom that enables him to recognize and expose the many idolatries seducing the human heart and to refute the erroneous logic by which these idolatries are justified.

Jesus couples his words about serpentine wisdom with the advice to be "innocent as doves," reminding us that those who follow Jesus may indeed appear to be naïve in the eyes of the world because they reject its ways in pursuing their agenda. They are wise enough to see that these ways, which rely on deception, hate and violence, are counterproductive and that only love is powerful enough to defeat evil. Therefore, they eschew these means and as a result are judged to be naïve by the world.

The first part of this book, which describes and analyzes some of the crucial characteristics of our age, is an effort to take seriously Jesus' advice to be wise as serpents. The second part, the theological section of the book, might be considered reflections on the second half of Jesus' advice in Matthew 10:16—to be "innocent as doves." Its purpose is to consider how Christians, once they become wise as serpents, can continue to pursue the nonviolent way of love and yet be not only faithful but powerful in effecting change in the world.

PART ONE

THE SOCIAL REALITY
OF OUR TIME

1

SERPENTINE WISDOM
IN AN AGE OF
CRISIS

Ours is an age of profound social crisis.

To be sure, history by its very nature offers periods of relative stability, alternating with periods of great social unrest, instability, change and crisis. Yet many have noted that the crisis before which we stand, while sharing many of the characteristics of earlier crises, is in some respects unprecedented. As Mexican social scientist Velaquez has said, "Today's crisis is different from any in previous history because it is global, progressive and could possibly be terminal."[1]

There is an external or structural dimension to the contemporary crisis. It is a crisis in human social systems. Today's social systems, developed in an earlier and simpler time, are no longer adequate to deal with today's problems. Because of the fundamental importance of this structural dimension of today's crisis, its resolution requires deep and radical changes in human social systems.

There is another, equally important side to today's crisis—the internal, psychological and spiritual side. The human psyche, on both the conscious and unconscious levels, is itself in crisis. Many ancient and common human experiences, which formed the images through which the psyche understood itself in relationship to the world, are less available today. Interactions between the psyche and the natural environment, which provided these experiences and images, are being replaced by interactions between the psyche and an artificial, technological environment. Myths and visions that gave meaning and direction to human experience and activity have been discredited and rendered impotent by the triumph of a materialistic and mechanistic world view and by its technological and manipulative approach to life. A famine of the spirit in our age hurtles the collective human psyche into a spiritual crisis of global proportions. The psyche wanders aimlessly in the desert of mechanistic materialism, bereft of any sense of meaning or belonging, cut off from its past, deprived of community, unsure of its identity and without any vision capable of leading it into the future.

The interior crisis of the psyche parallels the exterior crisis in human systems and is, perhaps, even more serious. Without a spiritual vision to guide us, it is unlikely that we will be able to move beyond the present critical situation that threatens our very existence on earth. As the Seer said, "Without a vision, the people get out of hand" (Prov. 29:18, Jerusalem Bible). On the other hand, because Christian faith in the incarnation perceives reality as made up of an inner or spiritual side and an outer or material one that are inextricably joined, and because it understands salvation holistically, from the perspective of Christian faith the inner and the outer dimensions of the present crisis must be approached and resolved together. The crisis in human systems cannot be resolved unless the spiritual crisis of the collective psyche is overcome. Equally true, resolution of the spiritual crisis must be accompanied by progress in solving the crisis in human social systems. The mission of Christians and the church is to lift up and live out their gospel vision of reality as one undivided whole and to proclaim and embody its message of holistic salvation in a way that manifests the relevance of this vision and message for today's world. To perform this mission, however, we need to understand more specifically the nature of the contemporary global crisis.

THE SOCIAL CRISIS: REVOLUTIONS
OF THE WORLD'S OPPRESSED

Observers of our age have long been aware of the many voices throughout the world being raised by and in behalf of the world's oppressed and marginalized peoples and of the many revolutionary movements that have arisen with the goal of obtaining, by persuasion if possible, by force if necessary, the rights of these groups. This revolutionary action on behalf of the world's oppressed is one of the most characteristic and widespread phenomena of our time. While uprisings of the oppressed have occurred throughout history, the revolutionary activity of today's oppressed and the consciousness out of which their actions proceed are in some ways unique.

One unique factor of today's uprisings is the existence of a powerful, persuasive and widely disseminated revolutionary ideology—Marxism—and of a method of social analysis that, although originated by Karl Marx and associated with Marxism, is employed by many non-Marxist scholars. Marxist ideology has convinced many of the poor and oppressed that their condition is not merely the result of their own vices but of the greed of the elite and its control of the economy. This class writes the rules by which the economy operates, thereby ensuring its own well-being, often to the detriment of nonpropertied workers. Marxist analysis has persuaded even many non-Marxists of its considerable truth. As a philosophy and a method of analysis, Marxism has influenced many philosophical, ethical and religious systems, increasing their awareness of the relationship between economic power, on the one hand, and economic justice on the other. Marxism has affected Christianity dramatically, making it more aware of the bias in favor of the poor that is at the heart of the Bible and the Christian tradition.[2]

A second unique factor of today's revolutionary consciousness and activity is its global dimension.[3] For the first time, a worldwide sense of solidarity is emerging among oppressed people, and a global political movement by and on behalf of the oppressed has developed. Here again, Marxism no doubt has played an important role through its efforts to inculcate a sense of solidarity among the oppressed. This growing unity is also a result of modern communications technology, which allows the rapid global spread of information, experience and insights.

A third unique factor is the dominance of a new world view, which could be called "evolutionary" or "developmental" and which has displaced in human consciousness the static view that prevailed through most of history. In that static view, the world has a fixed hierarchical order, established once and for all by God, who assigns everything and everyone a place to occupy and a duty to perform. One's moral and religious responsibility is to accept without question one's assigned place in this divinely established order, to fit into that order, and to perform to the best of one's ability one's assigned duty there. In the evolutionary view, the world is in an open-ended process of becoming. Movement and change are the fundamental characteristics of reality, and this movement is often understood teleologically, that is, as moving toward a goal. The goal itself is understood differently by each philosophy or religion—as a higher level of being, greater love, higher consciousness, or more comprehensive unity. But one's moral and religious responsibility, according to the evolutionary perspective, is consistent: to discern the direction of the world's development and work to further it.[4] For Christians, God is the chief actor in this evolutionary process.

This new world view awakens an awareness that change is possible, even inevitable, and that individuals can influence the direction of this change so as to ensure a better future for themselves and the world. Most importantly, it fosters belief in the moral and religious duty of people to work to bring about these changes. The writing of Jesuit priest and paleontologist Pierre Teilhard de Chardin is an example of this evolutionary world view interpreted from the point of view of Christian faith, as is the recent work of German biblical scholar Gerd Theissen.[5] People who view the world from this moral or religious perspective are less likely to accept oppression and exploitation as part of the eternally decreed order of things. On the contrary, they are likely to feel themselves called to eliminate exploitation and oppression so as to move the world toward greater justice. There are, of course, different views as to method and as to what a more just and humane society would look like. But there appears to be a growing consensus that such a society would surely be characterized by a more equal distribution of the world's power and wealth; by less reliance on violence to ensure order, provide security and achieve justice; and by a more responsible relationship to nature. Growing also is consensus that such changes cannot be made without radical changes in social attitudes and institutions.

An increasing number of Christian theologians and believers today are persuaded that the evolutionary world view is more compatible with biblical faith than is the static view of reality to which the church was historically wed. This static view, with its hierarchical and dualistic associations, is more closely related to Greek philosophy and to what Jürgen Moltmann calls "epiphany religions"[6] than to biblical faith. Many Christians are also concluding that an authentically Christian ethic is more compatible with the modern evolutionary or revolutionary ethic than with historically more influential conservative ethical approaches. After all, as José P. Miranda, among others, has shown, the Bible itself, especially its prophetic tradition and Jesus' teachings, is profoundly revolutionary in its critique of society. Miranda has also pointed out, however, that the revolution that Jesus envisions is far more radical than any secular revolutionary program, including Marxism, because it proposes the elimination of not only injustice and violence but also the ultimate evils of sin and death.[7] Such a revolution obviously is beyond the ability of human beings to achieve and can be achieved only by God. But God calls and empowers people to participate in this work. One of the great challenges facing Christians today is to understand properly the relationship between the ultimate and the penultimate, between God's work and humanity's work in giving birth to the new reality that Jesus referred to as the kingdom of God.[8]

Who are the oppressed groups rising up today, liberating themselves from dehumanizing conditions and demanding to participate in the drama of human history? The headlines of the times reveal that there are many. Any claim to a definitive list would be presumptuous, but certain groups are more significant, morally and politically, in the liberation struggle.

Economic Oppression

One of the largest and most severely oppressed groups is the poor. Concentrated in the Third World but also found in significant numbers in the United States, the poor live on the brink of physical extinction. They are deprived of even the most basic of human needs—food, clothing, shelter, clean water, medical care, education. The most vulnerable among them, children and the elderly, succumb to the mildest of viruses because their bodies, weakened by malnutrition, are too weak to fight. The life span of these groups is often little more than half that of the more affluent.

Clearly it can no longer be taken for granted that the poor will meekly resign themselves to their misery or blame themselves for it. With the help of passionate and prophetic leaders, including many in the church, the poor are coming to believe that their misery is neither the result of their sin nor the fate to which God has condemned them but is primarily the result of the political and economic systems of which they are a part, that these systems can be changed, and that they must engage in action to change them.[9] This understanding and the resulting hope transform the poor from passive and inert pawns of others' desires and actions into actors in their own right and on their own behalf.

Racial and Cultural Oppression

The European subjugation, colonization and enslavement of certain races and cultures created another group of oppressed people. Although the days of colonialism and slavery in the strict sense are over, their legacy lingers in the subtler forms of racial and cultural oppression, in discrimination and intimidation, and in economic exploitation of the Two-thirds World. Sophisticated philosophical, religious and ideological justifications for the oppression of "inferior" races and cultures still meet with acceptance in some quarters.

Such oppression occurs on a more global scale now in large part because of the extent of European colonization from the sixteenth through the nineteenth centuries. The oppressive policies and practices of European colonizers often resulted in genocide, at times unintentionally. In the New World especially, whole cultures, languages and peoples were destroyed.[10] Where that was not the case (as, for example, in Asia) Europeans failed to appreciate the value and beauty of native cultures far more ancient and in many respects more advanced and sophisticated than European culture. They violated the integrity of such cultures, shattered them beyond repair, trampled on the sensitivities of their peoples and indoctrinated conquered races to feel guilt for being dark skinned and belonging to a non-European culture. African slavery in the United

States is one of the most obscene chapters in the history of racial oppression. African slavery in the United States sought to reduce human beings to animals, stripping them of history, culture and even of language.[11] The survival of African slaves in America and their eventually successful effort to liberate themselves are tributes to the intellectual, spiritual and physical vigor of the African spirit and of the human spirit in general.

The uprising of culturally and racially oppressed groups all over the world evident today in the racial and ethnic disturbances in the Soviet Union is bringing an end to most of the overt colonialism that existed for 400 years. It has discredited the philosophical, ideological and religious systems that sought to justify cultural and racial oppression. It has ended legal segregation in the United States and brought some measure of justice to minorities throughout the nation. It has contributed to history two of the most important leaders of all time—Mahatma Gandhi and Martin Luther King, Jr. Indeed, the path explored by these great leaders in their philosophy and their political and social experiments may be the only one by which to move toward a more just and human future without destroying the world in the process.

In spite of these dramatic accomplishments, racial and cultural oppression linger on, often in increasingly subtle forms. In the Union of South Africa, however, the system of racial and cultural imperialism continues in statutory form and justifies itself on the basis of discredited racist ideologies. The global indignation generated by this system and the rebellion it has provoked offer hope that its end is in sight.

Oppression of Women

The women's movement is perhaps the most significant and profound of today's liberation movements and certainly potentially the largest. The women's movement is significant for the liberation movement in general because it is an uprising against the most ancient, universal and profound form of oppression. Oppression of women is part of all other forms of oppression. Modern studies have shown that it probably originated with the rise of "higher civilization" itself. To challenge the place assigned to women by society is, therefore, to challenge some of the deepest, most ancient and most powerful psychological and sociological patterns of the human species. Thus understanding the oppression of women helps uncover the dynamic operative in all forms of oppression.

Simone de Beauvoir in her definitive study, *The Second Sex*, says that the oppression of women is based on one of the most fundamental dialectics of human experience, the dialectic of subject and object or of self and other.[12] Early in the development of civilization, she argues, the male split apart this dialectic, creating a mythological dualism of self and other. Women were the group earliest and most consistently assigned the role of other (object), while the male took for himself the role of self (subject). The male's understanding of himself as self and his projection of the role of other onto the female is the basis of oppression of women throughout history.

As de Beauvoir suggests, modern human consciousness makes true mutuality in male–female relationships a real possibility today, but the persistence of this primitive mythology often prevents this possibility from being realized. The women's movement is an effort to overcome the influence of this self/other dualism in male–female relationships and to liberate both men and women to be fully human.

Once this dualism is established on the perceptual and conceptual levels, it is easy to see the self as master and assign the other the role of slave, and to apply the dualism to any number of groups.[13] Ironically, however, the very dualism by which I establish myself and my group as self/master over against another who is object/slave impoverishes and enslaves me, because it requires of me that I deny in myself all those qualities that I assign to the other and be always only pure self. I must avoid all self-understandings and behaviors that might be seen as weak, needy, womanish or vulnerable. I must not only oppress the other outside of myself, but must repress the other within myself in merciless and tyrannical fashion. The result is alienation and, in extreme cases, pathology. When whole societies understand and relate to themselves and their adversaries in these simplistic terms, the result is Nazism, Stalinism, or some other extremist and fanatical political philosophy and behavior of right or left. Recent examples are Iran, under the Ayatollah Khomeini, and Iraq, under Saddam Hussein. In our own country, the Ku Klux Klan, certain cults and various paramilitary organizations, mostly of right-wing orientation, manifest this self/other thinking to an alarming degree. In an age with more than enough weaponry to destroy the whole earth as a habitat for humankind, such social psychoses and the pathological political behavior to which they lead could prove fatal to humanity.

Religious Oppression

Oppression of religious minorities was more common in former times than it is today for several reasons. The ecumenical movement, for example, has dramatically reduced misunderstanding and hostility between religious communities. The secularization of society and the privatization of religion in the West have so greatly reduced religion's role in public life that there is little reason to oppress it, unless it attempts to function beyond the sphere assigned it by society or assumes a prophetic or countercultural form. The most overt religious oppression in our time has occurred in communist nations, which have confined religious communities to a narrow sphere of action. The oppression of prophetic religion in many Latin American nations, though less a matter of official policy, is often even more brutal than it has been in recent years in the Soviet Union, as Penny Lernoux has shown in her influential study of church/state conflict in those nations.[14] Even in the United States and other Western nations, various subtle but effective pressures are brought to bear on religious groups and expressions that are seen as too critical.

The persecution of Jews throughout the history of the "Christian" West, particularly in the most obscene of all historical events, the Holocaust,[15] is surely one of the darkest chapters in that history. Since the Holocaust, both Jews and Gentiles have worked to challenge anti-Semitic prejudices and attitudes and Christian churches have participated in these efforts. Pope John XXIII deserves special mention for his work to root anti-Semitism out of the Catholic church and its liturgical rites. In spite of these courageous and dedicated efforts, however, anti-Semitism still lingers and from time to time expresses itself in particularly repugnant ways.

Other oppressed groups are also rising up to challenge the attitudes and systems that oppress them. Some of the more visible groups include the handicapped, the aged, young people and children, and homosexuals.

Unique to our time is the global coming together and rising up of the numerous oppressed groups. This uprising reflects significant changes in the human psyche. It calls into question the elitist structures and processes of modern society that are inherited from an earlier time. It rejects the idea that these structures are part of a sacred and eternal metaphysical world order into which all people are called to fit. It reveals that today's social structures are out of touch with contemporary human consciousness and are unable to satisfy the longings or meet the needs of contemporary humanity. The oppressed and their supporters are not demanding a perfect world, a heaven on earth. But they do find the depth and scope of human misery today totally intolerable and, in light of present knowledge and technology, unnecessary. They blame this misery on an outmoded social order that is unable to cope with contemporary problems. Organizing themselves for action, they aim to change this order in whatever ways are necessary to make it more responsive to their needs. Irrational resistance to this increasingly powerful liberation movement serves only to make it more radical and violent and to ensure that change, which is sure to come, will be more vindictive and destructive.[16]

THE SYSTEMIC CRISIS:
GLOBAL HUMAN INTEGRATION

Developing global integration is a fact of life in our time; while it can be bemoaned or even resisted, it cannot be avoided or reversed. In their outstanding book, *Toward a Politics for the Planet Earth*, Harold and Margaret Sprout note, "It is becoming increasingly evident that interrelatedness, and the interdependencies that interrelatedness entails in the modern world, cannot be escaped."[17]

My arguments and supporting data in this section, unless other-wise indicated, are derived from their work.

Economic Integration

Perhaps the bottom line in this growing interrelatedness is global economic integration. There are a number of causes of this integration.

1. Economic specialization spawned by the industrial revolu-tion, which, for good or ill, encouraged some nations to specialize in the production of manufactured goods and others to provide raw materials and foodstuffs. Coloniza-tion forced this division of labor on the colonized territo-ries. One result is that producers of both raw materials and manufactured goods exist in a symbiotic relationship of unbalanced interdependence.

2. Growth in the external portions of the nations' economies. The larger the portion of a nation's gross national product (GNP) derived from imports and exports, the more inter-dependent the nation's economy is with the economies of other nations.

3. The growth of multinational corporations, which through their operations are largely responsible for the integration of the global political economy. Since the end of World War II, these corporations have moved beyond importing and exporting goods across national frontiers to organizing the production system itself on a global basis.[18] (I discuss some of the effects of this multinational-led economic inte-gration on the quality of life in chapter 2.)

4. The increasing importance of the international monetary system.

5. The growth in the transnational flow of money.

6. The increasingly important role played by the balance of payments in the world economy.

While each of these points is important, in the discussion that follows, I will focus on the role of multinational corporations.

The Role of Multinational Corporations

The power of the multinational corporation is far greater than the power of many of the small host nations in which it operates. Consequently, the sovereignty of even the largest and most powerful nations is often undermined by the maneuvers of these international conglomerates. In his book *Global Reach*, a study of the role played by multinational corporations in the global economy, Richard Barnet, political commentator and author of numerous books, says, "Large corporations plan centrally and act globally and nation states do not. It is this difference that puts government at a disadvantage in trying to keep up with and control the activities of global corporations." At the end of his analysis, Barnet concludes, "The globalization of the world political economy and the developing managerial crisis of the nation state are creating the necessity and perhaps the political foundations as well as the process of planetary reorganization."[19]

Alvin Toffler compares this crisis with the one the feudal fief faced as a result of the development of the technologies that climaxed in the Industrial Revolution. In order for these new technologies to function at full capacity and profitability, local and regional economies had to be integrated into economies of scale, because these technologies required a large market area. At the beginning of the modern period this meant, for the most part, national economies. The pressure for economic integration exerted on the politically decentralized feudal system by the developing technology of the Industrial Revolution was, in Toffler's opinion, one of the main causes of the demise of feudalism and the development of the nation-state. Toffler believes that decentralized, cybernetically based, low-energy third-wave technology is in turn eroding the independence of national economies by strengthening both local and regional economies on the one hand and the international economy on the other; it is in the process undermining the political economy of the nation-state and therefore the nation-state system itself and laying the economic foundations for global economic integration. According to Toffler, "Tightened economic linkages between nations make it virtually impossible for any individual national government to manage its own economy independently."[20] In the words of French political thinker Denis de Rougemont, "The nation state, which regards itself as absolutely sovereign, is obviously too small to play a real role at the global level today and in the future."[21]

The economic interdependence that is developing as a result of the integration of the global economy will be examined in more detail in chapter 2, where I evaluate it from the perspective of the question of economic justice: Who gains and who loses?

Psychological Integration

The psychological integration of humanity is another factor contributing to the erosion of the nation-state system's viability and power. While as late as the early nineteenth century psychological isolation of nations from one another was the rule, the opposite is more and more the case today.[22] Sophisticated communications technology, much of it by satellite, already penetrates the psychological isolation of every nation, subjecting each nation's citizenry to a critique from abroad of its national ideologies and policies. Such penetration can be expected to increase in the years ahead.[23]

Such "information invasions" weaken the power of a nation to isolate its citizens psychologically, to form and manipulate their psyches according to an official, government-approved plan, and to control and predict their political attitudes and behaviors. They also contribute to the emergence of a global perspective among more informed and reflective groups within all nations. In the consciousness of such groups, the narrow and fanatic national patriotisms of the past are being subordinated to and integrated within a broader "humatriotic" loyalty.[24]

Political Integration

The most dramatic and obvious sign of global human integration is a negative one—weapons of unlimited power, against which no nation can any longer defend itself. It is indeed ironic that this ultimate threat to the nation-state system should result from weapons that the nations developed to ensure their survival.

An advance in weapons technology, the gunpowder revolution of the fourteenth and fifteenth centuries, was an important cause of the emergence of the nation-state system of international politics. The feudal lords were unable to defend their territories against mobile artillery, and the feudal system collapsed. As I noted earlier, economic forces had already undermined the economic foundations of feudalism, just as today they are undermining the nation-states. While other technological developments of the time undoubtedly also played a role in undermining feudalism, the revolution in weapons was a key factor in bringing down the feudal system. Very quickly, indefensible feudal fiefs became integrated into larger, defensible political units, the emerging nation-states.

Once established, nation-states sought to develop the strongest possible defense systems against other nations. Natural defenses such as oceans, mountains and rivers were considered to be the best. Natural defenses were strengthened by strategic fortification. Geographic space became a key defense resource, one which took on increasing importance over time. By the end of World War I, it had become obvious that, in light of the existing weaponry, only the largest nations were viable. Successful defense against the weapons of the early twentieth century required that a nation be able to retreat under attack, regroup its forces, entice the enemy to move deep within its territory and far from its own sources of supply, and then counterattack.

> The expanding firepower and mobility of weapons were fatally eroding the military security of all but the very largest countries. A long sequence of inventions had raised the destructive capability of a single soldier by several orders of magnitude. Railroads, more and better roads, and more reliable and capacious overland vehicles had given unprecedented mobility to this expanding firepower. Development of marine mines, automotive torpedoes and submarines undermined the previously strong, natural defenses of insular countries. Aircraft foreshadowed the possibility of overlapping the most strongly defended land and sea frontiers.[25]

The continued development of aircraft and above all the introduction of offensive weapons such as intercontinental ballistic missiles and thermonuclear bombs mean that today no nation, however large or strong, is able to defend its territory from annihilating attack. More importantly, many scientists, such as those associated with the Union of Concerned Scientists, are convinced that an effective defense against these modern weapons is in principle impossible. In their view, offensive weapons systems have completely overwhelmed defensive ones.

The Star Wars debate illustrates this problem. A defensive system such as that envisioned by Star Wars is enormously expensive and is never fail-safe. In addition, whatever protection it may provide can be significantly reduced by the relatively simple and inexpensive strategy of increasing the number of offensive weapons beyond that with which the defensive system can cope. On the other hand, the enormous destructive capacity of modern nuclear, biological and chemical weaponry means that nothing short of a fail-safe defense can provide adequate protection to a nation and its people.

In light of this dilemma, true security in the late twentieth century must be sought not in multiplying offensive and defensive weapons systems, but in arms reduction and in the development of a new world order which sees national security in the context of global security and develops alternatives to war as a means of dealing with conflict. The ending of the Cold War, the unprecedented multilateral response to Iraq's invasion of Kuwait and the role of the United Nations in the Persian Gulf crisis could herald the beginning of a new world order in which multilateral cooperation replaces unilateral confrontation and options to war are developed and experimented with. It could also be a step toward replacing national military action with United Nations military action aimed not at territorial conquest but at the enforcement of international law.

The Sprouts have argued that the impact of developments in weapons technology on the nation-state system is "reminiscent of the destructive impact of the gunpowder revolution on medieval castles and walled towns."[26] If this is true, then the nation-states of today are as powerless against modern weapons as the feudal fief was against the weapons devised and deployed in the fifteenth century, and the nation-state system is doomed. Military and political leaders who seek to defend this anachronistic system by playing to nationalistic chauvinism and by increasing the defense budget are the Don Quixotes of the modern age. They are far more dangerous than Cervantes's character, however, because they have the power literally to destroy the future of humanity on this planet.

Few people, however, are predicting the immediate demise of the nation-state because "institutions tend to live on long after they have ceased to perform the essential functions for which they were created."[27] Indeed, according to sociologist Robert K. Merton, "Any attempt to eliminate an existing social structure without providing adequate alternative structures for fulfilling the functions previously fulfilled by the abolished organization is doomed to failure."[28] Merton goes on to point out, however, that "since there may be a range of ways in which a particular functional need may be fulfilled, we should look for functional alternatives," which "unfreeze[s] the identity of the existent and the inevitable."[29]

Functional Integration

In spite of the undeniable progressive integration of the human community on the functional level, the human psyche and imagination remain largely crippled and imprisoned by absolutized political loyalties. This enables nations to maintain their claim to absolute sovereignty, thereby preventing the development of a global authority and global institutions capable of ordering the life of the global community on the basis of reason and law. It is this contradiction between integration on the functional level and fragmentation on the institutional and to some extent the psychological levels that poses an increasingly serious threat to human well-being and even survival on the planet earth.

THE ENVIRONMENTAL CRISIS:
DOMINATION VERSUS STEWARDSHIP

From prehistoric times, people and societies have damaged their environments, sometimes so seriously that their culture collapsed or they were forced to seek a new environment. In the past, such damage affected primarily the society that inflicted it, and over time, nature was often able to recover. Today, however, the increased human population and the enormous power of modern technology mean that ecological damage caused by one society's mismanagement can affect the global environment and the quality of life of all nations.[30] Often, reversing or halting ecological damage requires the actions of many nations, and sometimes, as in the case of radioactive pollution, only time will reverse damage.

The management of our oceans illustrates how critical global ecological stewardship has become to future human welfare. The ocean supplies 70 percent of the free oxygen required for the survival of oxygen-breathing organisms. Increasingly, research has shown that through the application of various technologies, including ocean farming, the ocean could supply a far larger share of the needed protein for the human diet. The ocean, moreover, contains rich supplies of minerals, oil, gas, and coal. Only recently, as resources on land are being exhausted, has there been a need to utilize these riches of the seas, and only recently have technologies been developed that make the extraction of these ocean resources possible. The application of these powerful technologies must be carefully managed lest the global ocean become a dead sea. The drastic depletion of free oxygen in the atmosphere could mean the extinction of the human species and other oxygen-breathing species. Ecologically responsible use of the oceans' resources requires global cooperation and legal codes, as well as the creation of global agencies and institutions to enforce these laws and to regulate the management of the oceans in the interests of the global community. Morally responsible management of the oceans' resources requires that the wealth generated by these resources be equitably distributed rather than appropriated by the militarily and technologically strong nations. Such equitable distribution can only be ensured by a global authority that does not yet exist.

The global ecosystem is the ultimate context within which all other critical issues facing humanity must be understood and resolved. Even human social systems—political, economic, intellectual, cultural, scientific and technological—are part of all-embracing ecosystems and must move toward harmony with the principles and rhythms of this system. The human psyche must be converted from an engineering paradigm to an ecological paradigm. This does not mean that we must reject modern technology or abandon the quest for technological progress. It does mean, however, that technologies must respect and be integrated into the cyclical and renewing rhythms of the natural ecosystem. Only then will the technologies, the human communities they serve, and nature, on which these communities depend, be sustainable. Acknowledging the necessity of such integration does not mean denying all belief in evolutionary, teleological or linear progress. Technological progress and a recognition of the connection between humanity and nature are not incompatible. Even so enthusiastic a believer in the importance of technology as Karl Marx recognized our absolute dependence on nature, which he called the "inorganic body of man,"[31] and thus implicitly affirmed the necessity of technology's existing in harmony with nature. Our task is to structure appropriately the relationship between the linear, teleological movement of technology, history and evolution, and the self-renewing cycles of nature upon which all life on earth ultimately depends.

Many feminists see a relationship between what the Sprouts call the "ecological paradigm" and feminism. They note the need to move away from an attitude of domination, exploitation and manipulation of nature toward an attitude of nurturing and care-taking.[32]

Though the engineering model has made important contributions to human development and no doubt has a continuing role to play in human affairs, in light of the enormous power of modern technology, especially weapons technology, it may well prove disastrous if it remains the dominant model guiding human behavior in our time. The ecological paradigm could better guide contemporary social reconstruction.

THE SPIRITUAL CRISIS: THE DEMISE
OF DOMINANT INTELLECTUAL
AND SPIRITUAL VISIONS

Most significantly, ours is a time of spiritual crisis. The religious visions of the past that inspired and guided the individual and the collective psyche have lost much of their power. A variety of explanations have been offered for this phenomenon.

Acculturation

As I have noted, our age is characterized by frequent interaction between cultures and societies, by the progressive integration of the human community, and by the gradual emergence of a global culture and consciousness. One result of these developments is a heightened awareness of the relativity of specific cultures and cultural perspectives and the consequent quest for a universal vision. The world's major religions, however, have evolved within and become expressions of particular cultures. Their ways of understanding and relating to reality, including "ultimate" reality or God, as well as their myths, images, cultic practices and spiritualities, are largely religious expressions of a particular culture. This limits their ability to perceive reality as a whole and to articulate and incarnate a universal vision capable of inspiring and guiding humanity to global integration. Today's religions are faced with a crisis similar to the one the Olympian religion of Greece and Rome faced just before the time of Jesus. Although its spiritual vision was adequate to inspire and energize the life of the Greek city-states and early Rome, it was too culturally bound and parochial to provide the more cosmic vision needed to sustain the life of the cosmopolitan empires of Alexander and Caesar. Christianity eventually supplied that vision to the ancient Greco-Roman culture. It can do this for the modern age, however, only if it is able to transcend the particular cultural forms in which it has been expressed and incarnate itself in a form that relates to and interprets the experience of all cultures.[33]

Challenged by Third World theologians, many Christian theologians and leaders have become aware of Christianity's identification with Western culture and that Christianity is at times even presented as a national religion or as American civil religion.[34] The challenge to transcend particular cultural perspectives can provoke Christians to heighten their awareness of the distinction and tension between Christ and culture and to discern more clearly the essence of the Christian vision as distinct from the forms in which it has been expressed. I am convinced that this "core" vision, which can never be articulated once and for all but which we must always be striving to perceive and express, is far more universal than the various acculturated expressions of it and that it can be more clearly perceived through global dialogue.

If Christianity is to answer the cries of our time for a universal spiritual vision, it must free itself from captivity to Western culture and return to its origin, its experience of God in Jesus of

Nazareth. It is this experience, not the culturally determined interpretations of it, that must be proclaimed to the races, nations and
cultures of humanity. These groups must be free to interpret this
experience in the context of their own histories and cultures while
taking into consideration existing Western interpretations.

Interpretation

A second cause of the decline in Christianity's influence is the
dependence of Christian imagery and language on anachronistic
world views that sever Christianity from contemporary life and
experience. Interpretation based on such archaic views undermines
the ability of Christianity to captivate the modern mind, heart and
imagination, inspire the modern spirit, and channel the energies of
modern humanity into the common and urgent project of rebuild-
ing the earth. Christianity must free itself from dependence on
antiquated world views if it is to connect with the modern spirit
and influence the course of history.

Rudolf Bultmann attempted to address this problem by a process of reinterpretation that he called "demythologization."[35] He
believed that orthodox Christian doctrines were understandable
only in relationship to the ancient world's model of a three-storied
universe. Because we no longer picture the world in terms of this
model, these doctrines no longer make sense. Bultmann insisted
that Christian faith must be reformulated in terms of modern
humanity's understanding of reality. In his efforts to construct such
a demythologized theology, Bultmann relied heavily on the philosophy of Martin Heidegger.

Bultmann rightly identified a major problem faced by Christianity in the modern world and boldly addressed it, but his
demythologization program has many weaknesses. His suggestion
that Christian doctrines are dependent on a three-storied universe
is an oversimplification, and his understanding of mythology is
deficient. Another serious problem is Bultmann's unquestioning
acceptance of a Newtonian world view and his presupposition that
the Christian faith must be expressed in ways that do not violate
the principles of Newtonian physics. This presupposition rules out
from the very beginning some of the most important assertions
about reality that the Bible makes, including the New Testament's
understanding of the resurrection. Moreover, to insist that Chris-

tian faith be expressed in a way that does not violate a Newtonian model of reality is to make it dependent again on a world view that in light of the work of Einstein and quantum physics is already outdated.

Finally, Bultmann's very notion of a demythologized interpretation of Christianity should be challenged. Modern interpretations of the Christian faith should help people make sense of the whole of reality and of their own lives in relation to the whole and should inform the values and influence the behaviors of individuals and societies. In order to do this, these interpretations must relate to mythopoeic models of reality, for it is precisely such models that enable us to make sense of reality. What we need is not a demythologized but a remythologized interpretation of Christianity, that is, one that relates to a contemporary mythopoeic model of reality rather than an ancient one. In spite of his claim to demythologize Christianity, Bultmann in fact remythologized it by substituting a Heideggerian mythology of existence for earlier mythologies. Heideggerian mythology, however, is even less able to communicate Christian faith than the ancient mythologies reflected in the Bible. Heidegger and existentialism in general tend to reduce the world to one dimension—the individual's experience of his or her existence in the world. Existentialism offers an interpretation of human existence but is not really interested in the cosmos as such, in which it can find little or no meaning. Therefore it is not capable of developing a cosmology or a theology of creation, nor is it able to speak of God in anything like a biblical way. Its emphasis on individual experience also makes it virtually impossible for existentialism to express the communal and corporate essence of Christian life and faith or to develop a meaningful understanding of the church. The inadequacy of Heideggerian philosophy is therefore the primary problem with Bultmann's theology. It enables him to say a few things well and powerfully but makes even the utterance of other things, some of them very important to Christian faith, impossible.

Teilhard de Chardin, Gerd Theissen and process theologians such as John Cobb, David Ray Griffin, W. Norman Pittenger, and Ewart Cousins have chosen a more comprehensive model on which to base their reinterpretation of Christianity. The mythopoeic model that informs their theology is the evolutionary world view, which furnishes so much of the imagery through which the modern psyche interprets and relates to the world. The Marxist mythology of liberation theology is also more comprehensive than existentialism and, if one takes into consideration such writings as Friedrich Engels's *Dialectics of Nature*,[36] more closely related to the model of the process theologians than might at first be thought. Indeed, the relationship between matter and spirit and the developmentalism of this early writing of Engels is remarkably similar to some of the thoughts of Teilhard de Chardin in *The Phenomenon of Man*, although there is not likely to have been any direct influence.

An adequate biblical and theological hermeneutic today must be eclectic in the sense that it incorporates insights from all the above-mentioned sources as well as existentialism, structuralism, phenomenology, personalism, positivism and others.

Institutionalization

As French philosopher Henri Bergson has pointed out, the initial vitality, energy and missionary zeal of religions subside as institutionalization sets in.[37] Inasmuch as institutions and structures are essential for the survival of a religious community and movement, such a process is both inevitable and desirable. Over time, however, the institutions, structures, doctrines and rituals created by a religion tend to undermine its charismatic life and energy and transform what was once a movement in the world into a religious institution preoccupied with its own institutional interests and alienated from life in the world. Secular life, however, continues to develop and evolve. Religion, isolated from secular society by its confinement to a religious institution and by its preoccupation with the concerns of that institution, is little interested in and affected by social, political, intellectual, artistic and spiritual developments. Because of its institutional isolation, its impact on such developments also continuously wanes. Sensing its growing alienation from, irrelevance to, and marginalization by the world, institutional Christianity may make efforts to rehabilitate itself. It may seek, for example, to accommodate itself to some extent to the world in order to overcome its marginalization and reassert its influence. Such efforts, however, are motivated by institutional, not authentically religious, concerns. They are essentially attempts to maintain or reestablish the leading role of a religious institution in the world and are therefore often politically or economically rather than religiously motivated. This approach makes the problem worse because it is the overinstitutionalizing of Christianity that alienated it from the world in the first place. Worst of all, these efforts may block the path to true religious renewal or conversion by making a religious institution rather than God or Jesus Christ the center of concern. This was precisely the problem Jesus confronted in his struggle with the established religion of his time and society. Until the institutional church is prepared to die to itself for Jesus' sake, until, like John the Baptist, it is prepared to point to Jesus and say "he must increase, but we must decrease" (see John 3:30), no genuine rebirth of Christianity or powerful Christian vision is possible. Without such a vision the church will not have much to contribute to the resolution of the world's spiritual crisis.

THE FORCES OF KNOWLEDGE
AND TECHNOLOGY

Ours is an age of crisis in human affairs. Behind the various dimensions of this crisis lie two modern developments—the force of the rapidly increasing body of knowledge available to humanity and the rapidly developing technology based upon it.

Increasing knowledge played an important role in the emergence of the evolutionary world view, which sees change as the fundamental characteristic of all things. Knowledge and technology also contributed to the formation of the revolutionary consciousness behind today's uprisings among the oppressed and to the increasing integration of the global human community as well as to the severity of the environmental crisis. They have also discredited and displaced the world views that the world's major religions relied on to articulate their beliefs, and they have created a new world in which religion, for so long preoccupied with its own institutional concerns, is barely a part. All of these intellectual, scientific and technological developments confront Christianity with an enormous challenge in terms of relating to the modern age. Chapters 2 and 3 are an effort to understand this age more clearly. Chapters 4 through 7 are offered as a modest attempt to address theologically the challenge with which this age presents us.

2

THE DYNAMICS OF
UNDERDEVELOPMENT

In this chapter I attempt to shed some light on the crisis in global economic systems by discussing in some detail the structural dynamics contributing to the enormous economic inequities characteristic of our world. Basic to discussions of economic injustice are the categories First, Second, and Third Worlds.[1] The First World includes the United States, Western Europe, Japan, Australia, New Zealand and a few other highly industrialized and economically developed nations. The Second World consists of the countries of Eastern Europe and the Soviet Union. My focus in the following discussion is on the less-developed nations of the Third World. The source of my data, unless otherwise noted, is Michael P. Todaro's volume, *Economic Development in the Third World*.

The United Nations divides Third World nations into three groups: (1) the forty-two poorest or least-developed nations, sometimes referred to as the Fourth World; (2) the remaining non–oil-exporting nations; and (3) the less-developed oil-exporting nations.[2]

The Third World nations contain 76 percent of the world's population, but must subsist on only 27 percent of the world's income. The economic gap between the nations of the First and Third Worlds continues to widen. For example, from 1960 through

1982, the gap in gross national product (GNP) between First World and Third World nations widened at the rate of 2.3 percent per year. During this same period, the gap between First World and non–oil-exporting Third World nations in per capita income widened by 1.9 percent per year after adjusting to account for population growth. Within the less-developed countries, income distribution is far more unequal than in the developed countries.[3] Indeed, one sign of development seems to be a more equal distribution of income between groups within a nation.

In the 1980s, this enormous income gap between the rich and poor worlds and between the rich and the poor in the poor world resulted in a number of alarming statistics:

1. Approximately 1.2 billion people were living in absolute poverty, that is, subsisting on income below the international poverty line.

2. More than one billion people, one-third of them under two years of age, were malnourished. Many of the children suffer permanent brain damage because of a lack of proper nourishment in the womb and during infancy. They constitute a mentally deficient working class like the "Epsilons" in Aldous Huxley's *Brave New World*. Severe malnutrition also causes other physical damage, especially when suffered at an early age, and is responsible for the lethargic behavior sometimes observed among the destitute and often wrongly attributed to laziness.

3. The diets of more than 60 percent of the people of Africa and Asia barely meet minimum calorie requirements.

4. In 1984, life expectancy in the least-developed nations averaged forty-nine years, in the less-developed countries fifty-seven, and in the developed countries seventy-two. Approximately 70 percent of deaths recorded each year in the Third World are due to hunger or to problems arising from hunger.[4]

5. In 1984, infant mortality in the least-developed nations averaged 124 per 1,000, in the less-developed countries 86 per 1,000, and in the developed countries 18 per 1,000.

6. In the poorest countries, 25 percent of children die before reaching the age of five.[5]
7. During the early 1980s, in the least-developed countries the doctor/patient ratio was 9.7 per 100,000; in the developed countries it was 158 per 100,000. The few doctors practicing in Third World nations are clustered in cities, leaving the countryside without adequate medical services.
8. The literacy rate in the least-developed countries is 37 percent, in the less-developed countries 63 percent, and in the developed countries 97 percent.
9. The United States, with approximately 6 percent of the world's population, consumes as much as 40 percent of the world's resources, including 33 percent of the world's oil and 63 percent of its natural gas.[6] The people of the United States use more energy for air conditioning alone than the one billion people of China use for all purposes.
10. In one year, the average American consumes as many resources as it would take to sustain ninety Indians.[7]

To make these statistics still more concrete, let's focus on El Salvador, a country that is much in the news in connection with public debate over the United States' Central America policy. In El Salvador, 95 percent of the people are without running water in their homes and 75 percent have no access to safe drinking water. Eighty percent do not have toilets of any kind, 71 percent of the rural and 50 percent of the urban work force is unemployed and 40 percent of the total population and 75 percent of the children are severely malnourished.[8] Indeed, the average domestic house cat in the United States eats more beef than the average person in El Salvador.[9] Thirty-five percent of the people of El Salvador are illiterate.[10] This enormous poverty is rooted not in the natural conditions of the country but in the political and economic structures which ensure that the resources of the country will remain in the hands of the elite. The richest fifth of the population receives two-thirds of the income while the poorest fifth receives 2 percent,[11] and 1 percent of the farms of the nation comprise 71 percent of the total farmland.[12] The annual per capita income in El Salvador is $710.[13]

These statistics and the human misery they represent are heartbreaking. The church has always sought to minister to this misery but has often responded only with charity. Charity is an essential response of Christian faith to human misery. Indeed, without charity, Christian faith and spiritual life atrophy and die, because to turn away from suffering is to turn away from God, as Jesus tells us in the parable of the sheep and the goats (Matt. 25:31-46). And charity does, in fact, alleviate misery, perhaps even enabling some to escape the cycle of poverty, malnutrition, misery and death to which circumstances otherwise condemn them. But charity, as individual and voluntary acts of mercy, cannot change fundamentally the global economic reality characterized by enormous discrepancies in wealth and power. Only radical structural changes aimed at greater equality in the distribution of power and wealth can accomplish this. Such structural changes are possible only through sustained and serious political action. Because the mission of Christians and the church includes the call to work for the total well-being of all people in this world, the church must be committed to and involved in this action.

To work responsibly and effectively for justice in the world requires an accumulation of what I referred to in chapter 1 as serpentine wisdom. It requires of concerned people, Christian and non-Christian alike, that they probe beneath the surface of the facts and discover the underlying causes. Such probing reveals that much of the human misery I have described is caused by economic and political systems that are controlled by a small elite and do not respond to the needs and wants of the masses. Paul included such social systems among the "principalities and powers" (Eph. 3:10). Serpentine wisdom enables us to understand these systems and how they work. Faith enables us to critique them on the basis of Christian beliefs and values, and provokes us to ask such questions as Who controls the system? Who makes the rules? Who benefits from them? Who suffers because of them? Aided by such questions and by social analysis, we will seek in this chapter to develop some worldly wisdom about the global economic system and to understand how it contributes to the suffering of the masses.

THEORIES OF DEVELOPMENT

There is general agreement among economists that the over-all cause of the widespread misery in the Third World is economic underdevelopment. If this is true, the cure for this misery is development. There are, however, strong disagreements among economists regarding the definition of development and various opinions about how best to promote it. Economists also differ in their understanding of what the chief obstacles to development are.

Stages-of-Growth Model

In the 1950s and early 1960s, development thinking was dominated by W. W. Rostow's "Stages of Growth" theory. This primarily economic theory taught that the right quantity and mixture of saving, investment and foreign aid were all that was necessary for development. The key to growth is savings. For development to take place, capital must be accumulated, mobilized and invested. The higher the rate of savings, the more money to be invested in development and the more rapid the development process. Such a theory led to development policies permitting the wealthy to retain a high portion of their income for accumulation in the belief that they would invest it in the development process, and that the benefits of this investment would then "trickle down" to the impoverished masses.

After ten to fifteen years of economic development policy based on the Stages of Growth theory, disillusionment began to set in; the policies were not succeeding. And even in those countries such as Brazil where development, defined in narrowly economic terms, did take place at rather astonishing rates, the misery of the masses was not alleviated but deepened. This disillusioning experience led to the emergence of the International Structuralist model of development.

International Structuralist Model

The International Structuralist model begins with a holistic definition of development: "Development must . . . be conceived of as a *multidimensional process involving major changes in social structures, popular attitudes, and national institutions, as well as the acceleration of economic growth, the reduction of inequality and the eradication of absolute poverty.*"[14] Here, noneconomic factors such as systems of land tenure and the flexibility or rigidity of economic and social classes are as important as the manipulation of strategic economic variables such as saving, investment and foreign exchange. Development so defined cannot be measured in strictly economic terms such as growth in savings, rate of investment, or growth in GNP or per capita income.

Many church leaders concerned about economic justice have adopted this structuralist definition of development. Pope Paul VI, in his important social encyclical, *Populorum Progressio*, spoke about "integral human development":

> The development of which we speak cannot be limited to mere economic growth. In order to be authentic, it must be complete: that is it has to promote the good of every person and of the whole person. As an eminent specialist has very rightly and emphatically declared, "we do not believe in separating the economic from the human nor development from the civilizations in which it exists!"[15]

In the same encyclical, the pope also affirmed that advocacy on behalf of integral development is a constitutive part of the life of faith and the mission of the church.

FROM ANALYSIS TO POLICY FORMULATION

Having articulated a holistic understanding of development, Michael P. Todaro proceeds to ask the question, "What policies would promote development understood in these terms?" Todaro's suggestions form the basis of our discussion of Third World and global economic policy.

Economic Policy in the Third World

Domestic economic policies aimed at promoting integral development must be concerned not only with the rate of growth in GNP and per capita income but also with the *character* of this growth and the question of who profits from it. Distribution of income is as important as income generation. Thus, policies should be designed to promote greater equality in income distribution.

The policies of many less-developed countries (LDCs) have done exactly the opposite! As a result, the effect of economic growth has too often been a decrease in the income of the poorest 40 to 60 percent of the people. Policies supposed to result in economic trickle down in fact had a trickle-up effect.[16]

Todaro proposes certain measures to promote greater equality of income in Third World nations:

1. Lower the cost of labor relative to capital to encourage greater use of labor as opposed to capital-intensive technologies, thus creating more jobs and alleviating the enormous underemployment and unemployment. Given the already low wages in many LDCs, this would mean higher cost for capital.

2. Redistribute present assets in capital and land. Because inequality in the distribution of wealth is a major cause of the unequal distribution of income, without redistribution of wealth no significant adjustment of income distribution can be effected. Such a policy may be anathema to laissez-faire capitalist ideologies, but has been advocated by, among others, Pope Paul VI, who stated, "The common good sometimes requires the expropriation of certain landed estates if they impede the general prosperity because they are extensive, unused or poorly used, or because they bring hardship to people or are detrimental to the interests of the country."[17]

3. Levy progressive taxes designed to achieve greater equality in income distribution through direct redistribution. Funds generated should be used for development projects designed to aid the poor and, in the process, provide them with meaningful jobs.

4. Increase the income of the poor through a welfare system. Projects designed to improve their living conditions in direct ways should be given high priority: sewage systems, safe water supplies, medical and educational services.

Economic policies designed to promote integral development must also address the problem of population growth. Certain First

World theoreticians such as Paul Ehrlich, Anne Ehrlich and Lester Brown tend to blame population growth for all economic and social evils. Some Third World economists, however, contend that population growth is a pseudo-issue used by the rich nations to avoid facing unpleasant questions about redistribution of power and wealth. Todaro does not share this view but he does insist that the population issue cannot be dealt with in isolation from other development issues. Using the history of today's developed nations as an example, he notes that a decrease in birth rates and therefore in population growth is a normal result of integral development. Todaro does not rule out direct population-control programs but suggests that such programs, if pursued in lieu of rather than as an integral part of an effective overall development policy, will be minimally effective in the long run. The best way to achieve population control is to integrate it into an overall development strategy.

Economic policies designed to promote integral development must be more concerned with increasing employment than output. This means the use of appropriate intermediate technologies that are labor intensive rather than capital-intensive high technologies. The opposite has often been the case, largely because technologies adopted by the Third World are developed in First World nations to fit First World economies and needs. Furthermore, these technologies are owned by First World corporations, which often charge exorbitant fees to Third World enterprises wanting to use them. This problem is rooted in the fact that 98 percent of all technical research takes place in developed countries. We must challenge the intellectuals and scientists of the Third World to develop technologies appropriate to the Third World social and economic realities and designed to solve Third World problems.

Economic policies to promote integral development in LDCs must give priority to the agricultural sector. (Except in China and to some extent in Tanzania, exactly the opposite has been the case in the development planning of Third World nations.) This is important for several reasons. First, in spite of massive urban migration, the majority of people in LDCs still live in rural areas. Second, self-sufficiency in food is important because excessive dependence on imported food is costly and renders LDCs vulnerable to political pressures from the First World. Finally, giving priority to agricultural policy can help overcome the discrepancy of quality of life on the land versus in the city. This discrepancy is the greatest cause of the massive migrations from rural areas to the city that are disrupting the social and economic life of the Third World. These migrations depopulate the land and undermine agricultural productivity. And by overpopulating the cities, they strain inadequate public services to the point of collapse.

Third World agricultural policy must be substantively formulated and implemented with the following goals:

1. Patterns of land ownership must be changed through expropriation and redistribution, particularly in Latin America where 1.3 percent of the landowners own 71.6 percent of all the land under cultivation. This land ownership pattern is called the "latifundia system." Latifundia are the large estates that were established in the colonial period and passed down from generation to generation. In Argentina, the average latifundium is 270 times larger than the average holding of the peasants, called a minifundium, and in Guatemala the ratio is 1,732 to 1. And there are a growing number of even smaller peasant holdings, called microfundia, in Latin America, 75,000 in Guatemala alone, for example. Todaro argues that the latifundia system must be ended if life on the land is to be substantially improved and rural and urban living standards are to be equalized.

2. Government programs designed to improve conditions and productivity in the agricultural sector must be made available to small landholders. Access to credit on nonexploitive terms, access to markets and inputs such as fertilizers, availability of technologies and agricultural expertise that government programs provide often come disproportionately to the wealthy and large landowners, further skewing the situation in their favor. Modern technologies are often too costly for small landowners, too complicated for them to use, and are, in any case, inappropriate for small holdings. Government planners must make valiant efforts to develop policies that benefit small landowners if these inequities are to be overcome.

3. High priority must be given to programs designed to bring
   such services as health care, education, roads, clean water
   and sewage systems to the rural sector. Such services presently are available only in the cities, and even then not for
   everyone.

The integral development of the Third World also requires
reevaluating the prevailing educational philosophy and practice.
The assumptions that the key to development lay in the education
of the people led Third World nations to invest enormous sums in
education. Unfortunately, the education model has been imported
from the West; it is an essentially elitist model that pays little
attention to the relationship between education and life, and education and the social situation. It is education for thinking rather
than education for living. The model assumes that the goal of
education is more education. But in the Third World, few students
get beyond primary school. Moreover, a disproportionate amount
of education funds supports university education for the elite, many
of whom then migrate to the First World where there are more
lucrative jobs. This elitist approach to education increases inequality and perpetuates poverty. Rather than this model, Third World
nations need an approach to education that emphasizes primary
education and prepares primary school pupils to solve the problems of peasant life in less-developed societies.[18]

The International Economic Order[19]

So far I have discussed the domestic economic policies of
Third World nations. But the economies of Third World nations are
part of a global economic order that is controlled by and operates
in the interests of the First World nations. The economies of Third
World nations are caught in a largely unhealthy dependency relationship, and the integral development of these nations requires
changes in the international economic order. If such changes prove
impossible, then Third World nations must break free of the international economic system. Suggested changes in the international
economic order that development economists as well as the United
Nations General Assembly call for include:

1. Developed countries (DCs) should eliminate trade barriers for processed goods from LDCs. This would encourage the development of manufacturing in LDCs by making their manufactured goods more competitive. Often LDCs may export their raw materials to DCs without paying a tariff, but if they process these goods before exporting them, a tariff is charged. Obviously these regulations protect the already strong industries of the First World and prevent potentially competitive industries in the Third World from developing. Instead of protecting workers whose jobs may be threatened by imports from LDCs through trade barriers, DCs should invest in retraining programs for those workers.

2. DCs should stop subsidizing their exporters. Subsidies artificially lower the prices of the DC's exports and give these goods an unfair advantage over goods produced domestically in LDCs. It becomes difficult for the fledgling Third World industries to market their products even in their own countries.

3. Multinational corporations in the LDCs must serve the development goals of the host country. Controlling these corporations' activities is difficult because of their size and power. Because they are often more powerful than the host countries, their activities can be regulated only if LDCs work together and if DCs cooperate or at least do not interfere in behalf of multinational corporations.

4. Third World nations must insist that the terms of aid be changed. Todaro urges cutting off all military aid and all aid from commercial sources, because the terms are often so unfavorable as to be exploitive. Only noncommercial aid given on concessional terms should be accepted, and quid pro quos should be minimal. DCs offer aid to LDCs to promote their own political and economic interests. Often this involves supporting unpopular and oppressive dictatorships that guarantee a favorable investment climate for First World economic interests—low (or no) taxes, minimal environmental regulations, political stability, minimal

regulation of corporate policy.[20] The demand for political stability by multinational corporations has been especially disastrous in the Third World. As Dom Helder Camara, Archbishop of Recife/Olinda in Brazil, has pointed out, it has led to the establishment of repressive regimes that seek to eliminate the possibility of every form of protest. Indeed, Camara believes that a true Nazism is arising in Latin America in the name of national security and anti-communism.[21]

At present, the DCs dictate the terms on which aid is granted, thereby ensuring they are repaid their aid money many times over. First, much of this aid is in the form of loans, to be repaid with interest (until recently, the LDCs had a good record of payment). Second, the terms of United States loans, for example, often require that the money be spent on United States goods. One result of these aid policies is that in recent years larger and larger amounts of capital have been transferred from the Third World to the First. Another result has been the increasingly unmanageable debt crisis into which many of the least-developed nations have fallen.[22]

Further suggestions for change in the international economic order are found in the proposal for a New International Economic Order introduced in the United Nations by the Group of Seventy-seven and passed by the Sixth Special Session of the United Nations General Assembly in 1974. Although the suggestions contained in this proposal, for the most part, have yet to be acted on and have encountered serious resistance from the First World, especially the United States, the United Nations' action was important because it raised the consciousness of the world regarding these issues and introduced important suggestions for reforming the international economic order. These suggestions are still being vigorously discussed.

Among the suggestions contained in the proposal for a New International Economic Order are the following:

1. Renegotiating existing LDC debts, with those of the poorest

countries being cancelled and those of the wealthier being consolidated and revised to offer more favorable terms.

2. Indexation, tying the price paid by DCs for raw materials and agricultural products to the price paid by LDCs for manufactured goods. This is an international version of parity.

3. The establishment of a common fund to be used to stabilize the prices of Third World products. In years of low prices, surplus goods would be bought up to establish buffer stockpiles, thus keeping prices stable; when the price of a given commodity rose above an agreed-upon amount, the buffer stock would be released to bring them down.

4. Greater power for LDCs in international lending institutions such as the International Monetary Fund and the World Bank.[23]

These and similar proposals for reform of the international and domestic economic orders are quite moderate and, for the most part, remain within the framework of a market economy. They are also supported by a growing number of development economists, sociologists, political scientists, social ethicists, international diplomats, theologians, church leaders and officers of international and church-related relief agencies. Philip Land, an economist and Jesuit theologian, has surveyed these proposals for reform of the economic order and demonstrates the broad consensus in support of these proposals.[24] Why, then, have at least some of the provisions called for in these proposals not been enacted?

THE POLITICS OF UNDERDEVELOPMENT

Strong resistance to these proposals by economic and political leaders in both Third and First World countries exists for both economic and ideological reasons. The proposals contradict the laissez-faire ideology of classical capitalism and threaten the power and interests of leaders. In fairness, it must also be admitted that, if not wisely implemented, these changes could cause major economic problems for all people and even under the best of circumstances would risk major disruptions in the world economy.

Pope Paul VI criticized this sort of resistance:

> The rule of free trade, taken by itself, is no longer able to govern international relations. . . . Prices which are freely set in the market place can produce unfair results. . . . An economy of exchange can no longer be based solely on the law of free competition, a law which in its turn too often creates an economic dictatorship. Freedom of trade is fair only if it is subject to the demands of justice.[25]

The Latin American bishops at their conference in Medellín went further in their critique of the international capitalist ideology and its resistance to reform:

> The principal guilt for the economic dependence of our countries rests with foreign powers inspired by uncontrolled desire for gain, which leads to economic dictatorship and the international imperialism of money.
>
> Another feature of this economic situation is our subjection to capital interests in foreign lands. In many cases, these foreign interests exercise unchecked control, their power continues to grow and they have no permanent interest in the countries of Latin America. Moreover, Latin American trade is jeopardized by its heavy dependence on the developed countries. They buy raw materials from Latin America at cheap prices and then sell manufactured products to Latin America at ever higher prices.[26]

They continued this line of thought at the Third Latin American Bishops Conference in Puebla, Mexico, in 1979.

The elites in First and Third World nations, in alliance with one another, have been quite successful in maintaining the political and economic status quo. Their success is, in part, due to the support of workers in the First World who are convinced that they derive some benefit from the existing system. Their hand has also been strengthened by the illiteracy and ignorance of Third World peasants, who until recently had only a vague idea as to what the cause of their misery was. Often, in fact, they tended to blame themselves, as they have long been taught to do. In Latin America, many church leaders, priests, pastors, nuns and educators have in recent years engaged the peasants in a process of "conscientization," a term coined by Brazilian educator Paulo Freire.[27] Conscientization is designed to teach peasants to read and write and, in the process, to help them gain an awareness that the causes of their misery are to be found in the national and international political and economic system of which they are a part. Basic Christian communities that have sprung up by the thousands throughout Latin America have incorporated this process into prayer, Bible study and eucharistic celebration. Through these communities, poor Latin Americans have learned to experience God as lover of the poor and champion of justice. They have also gained a new awareness of their own worth and dignity as children of God and have been empowered to come together as a community and engage in political action in behalf of social and economic justice.

As far back as the 1950s, this self-consciousness and political power of the poor began to make itself felt in the political arena. The poor, with the help of sensitive and sympathetic political and church leaders, began to threaten the power of ruling elites throughout the world and especially in Latin America. Through the political process, they began to elect reform-minded politicians. Unfortunately, the ruling class in these nations, with the aid of political and industrial leaders in the United States who saw their economic interests challenged, were able to persuade American officials that the reformists were communists, thus ensuring American military and economic assistance in their struggle to regain power.[28]

Jack Nelson Pallmeyer describes a CIA-organized and -led coup in 1954 that overthrew a democratically elected reformist government in Guatemala that was perceived as a threat to American economic interests, especially those of the United Fruit Company.

> In 1952, the United Fruit Company owned or controlled about 3 million acres of land worldwide, of which only about 241,000 acres were actually planted with crops. The rest was left idle or grazed by a few cattle to keep landless peasants from cultivating it. Thomas McCann, a former vice-president of United Fruit, describes the situation in Guatemala.
>
> "Guatemala was chosen as the site for the company's earliest development activities because a good portion of the country was prime banana land and also because at the time we entered Central America, Guatemala's government was the

region's weakest, most corrupt and most pliable." In short, the country offered an "ideal investment climate," and United Fruit's profits flourished for fifty years. Then something went wrong: a man named Jacob Arbenz became president.

United Fruit's problems actually began before the election of Jacob Arbenz. In 1944, General Jorge Ubico, a brutal dictator who played a central role in maintaining the ideal investment climate for the United Fruit Company, was overthrown. Ubico, who proudly compared himself to Hitler, banned labor unions, and declared the word "worker" subversive. Following Ubico's loss of power, Juan José Arevalo was elected president in a popular election. Arevalo abolished forced labor on the banana plantations, raised minimum wages to 26 cents a day, permitted unions, and began prying the Guatemalan economy from its near total dependency on United Fruit and other foreign corporations. In response to Arevalo's reforms, W. R. Grace and Pan American Airlines stopped promoting tourism, several oil companies discontinued prospecting, United Fruit restricted banana exports, the World Bank withheld loans, and the United States government, which accused Arevalo of being a communist, cut off military assistance.

In March of 1953, Jacob Arbenz Guzman, the democratically elected president whose principal concern was land reform, expropriated 234,000 uncultivated acres of land owned by United Fruit. Arbenz offered as compensation an amount of money equal to United Fruit's assessment of value for tax purposes.

On June 18, 1954, American pilots bombed Guatemala City. Arbenz was overthrown with weapons shipped on ships owned by United Fruit in a Central Intelligence Agency initiated coup. His replacement, Colonel Carlos Castillo Armas, was a graduate of the United States Command General Staff College at Fort Leavenworth, Kansas. He immediately returned United Fruit's expropriated land and abolished taxes on interest and dividends to foreign investors.

United Fruit Company had friends in high places. At the time of the American intervention, John Foster Dulles, a longtime legal advisor to the company, was US Secretary of State; his brother, Allen Dulles, was director of the CIA; Henry Cabot Lodge, a large stockholder and member of United Fruit Company's board of directors, was the US ambassador to the UN; John Moors Cabot, a large shareholder, an Assistant Secretary of State for Inter-American Affairs, and Walter Bedell Smith, a predecessor of Allen Dulles as director of the CIA, became president of the United Fruit Company after the Arbenz government was overthrown.[29]

American intervention throughout the world was intended to install or prop up governments that would ensure favorable investment climates for American economic interests. For example, the CIA mounted a saturation campaign against the moderately reformist, democratically elected regime of Julius Goulart in Brazil in 1962. The CIA paid for eighty radio programs and 300 hours of radio and television advertising, flooded the Brazilian press with CIA-produced editorials and information pieces, set up numerous billboard ads and printed pamphlets by the millions. Dozens of journalists were on its payroll for the campaign and edited a monthly magazine that was distributed free nationwide. It rented the editorial page of Rio de Janeiro's evening paper, *A Noite*, and subsidized the publication of numerous conservative books, which were distributed free with no indication of authorship.[30] These CIA-led efforts were successful in overthrowing the Goulart regime and replacing it with a brutal military dictatorship that held power in Brazil until 1986, when under pressure from the church, peasant groups, the United States and other sources, the military dictatorship agreed to the installation of a civilian government.

The United States Marine invasion of the Dominican Republic that overthrew the democratically elected government of Juan Bosch in 1965 is another example of American intervention on behalf of ruling elites.[31] But the classic example of American intervention to overthrow a democratically elected government perceived as a threat to economic interests occurred in Chile. Through a massive program of destabilization, in which ITT, Kennecott Copper, the State Department and the CIA cooperated, the government of Salvador Allende was undermined and then overthrown in a bloody coup in 1973, to be replaced by the brutally repressive military dictatorship of Augusto Pinochet.[32]

Norwegian peace researcher Johan Galtung offers an analysis of the dynamics at work in such political scenarios. According to Galtung, they are the dynamics of imperialism in its post-colonial form.[33] He believes that, in alliance with the elite in First World nations, the elites of the Third World maintain a control of the political and economic life of Third World nations, ensuring that the wealth of the nation will flow into their hands. They retain a large portion for themselves. Much of the remaining wealth passes into the First World countries, helping to maintain the standard of living to which the people of these nations have become accustomed.

If Galtung's analysis correctly illustrates the power relationships between first (center) and third (peripheral) nations and between elites and the masses within those nations, these relations reflect the classic self/other or master/slave relationships described in chapter 1. Such relationships are at the root of the economic and political injustices described in this chapter. Economic and political changes of the magnitude required to overcome these injustices will require significant changes in the power relationships between nations and groups within nations. One can only hope and pray that such changes can be accomplished with a minimum of violence, following a Gandhian pattern. The deep and wide-ranging changes that occurred in 1989 in Eastern Europe and the Soviet Union and were achieved largely through nonviolent action offer some hope for this.

3

THE NUCLEAR THREAT
TO SURVIVAL

To ensure the future of humanity, nations and their peoples must come to realize that, with the explosion of the first atomic bomb at the Trinity test site in Alamogordo, New Mexico, on July 16, 1945, a new era in human history began. Albert Einstein, the father of the nuclear age, frequently reminded us that the splitting of the atom confronted life on this planet with an unprecedented threat. Picking up on Einstein's warning, John Platt, a social scientist from the University of Michigan, articulated the thesis of this chapter when he said, "The one crisis that must be ranked at the top in total danger and imminence is the danger of large scale or total annihilation by nuclear escalation."[1]

Although recent events in international politics, above all glasnost and perestroika in the Soviet Union, have lessened the risk of nuclear war, the world remains a dangerous and unstable place, as recent developments in the Persian Gulf and the Middle East generally serve to remind us. The danger and instability which the planet faces are not likely to be significantly reduced so long as present arsenals of nuclear weapons remain in existence. Even if all the reductions presently under discussion in the START talks were achieved, enough weapons would remain to decimate the world.

My aim in this chapter is to make the reader more familiar

with the nature of nuclear weapons systems and thereby with the unprecedented scope and gravity of the threat they pose to the future of humanity. Perhaps the best way to begin a description of the destructive power of nuclear weapons is to consider the devastation effected on Hiroshima and Nagasaki by the only nuclear bombs ever used in war.[2]

THE FIRST GENERATION

The bombs exploded on Hiroshima and Nagasaki on August 6 and 9, 1945, were tiny fission weapons of between ten and fifteen kilotons of explosive power. Yet they instantaneously killed one hundred thousand people in Hiroshima and fifty thousand in Nagasaki. Perhaps an equal number died in the days, months and years following as a result of cell damage due to radiation. Fifteen years after the Hiroshima explosion, for example, an epidemic of leukemia occurred among survivors, who developed the disease at forty times the rate of the general population. One of these victims was a twelve-year-old girl about whom a poignant story titled "Sadako and the 1000 Paper Cranes" was written.[3]

The enormity of the breakthrough in death technology represented by Hiroshima is dramatically illustrated by Jonathan Schell, author of the bestselling book, *The Fate of the Earth*, who points out that the destructive power of the Hiroshima bomb, equivalent to fifteen tons of TNT, was produced by the conversion of one gram of matter into energy.[4]

SECOND GENERATION

The Hiroshima and Nagasaki bombs, however, were just the primitive first generation of nuclear weapons. Since 1945, single weapons 2,500 to 3,000 times as powerful have been tested. Such bombs are more powerful than the combined force of all non-nuclear explosions that have ever occurred. These huge thermonuclear weapons use bombs the size of the Hiroshima bomb as triggers.

By the end of 1985, the United States possessed approximately 32,000 nuclear weapons, 20,500 of which were tactical and

11,466 strategic. The Soviet Union possessed about 20,000 weapons, of which approximately 9,208 were strategic and the rest tactical.[5] Together, these two nations had the equivalent of approximately one million Hiroshima bombs, enough to kill every man, woman and child on earth eight times. Any discussion of the nuclear superiority of one side or the other must be evaluated within the context of the enormous overkill capacity on both sides.

The delivery systems for these bombs represent an even greater threat than the bombs themselves because they render an effective defense against these weapons virtually impossible (see my discussion in chap. 1). The bombs are deployed according to the so-called nuclear triad strategy, that is, on land-, sea- and air-based delivery systems. Fifty percent of all American weapons are deployed on Poseidon and Polaris submarines and are practically invulnerable to enemy attack. Poseidon submarines are capable of carrying 224 nuclear bombs each, every one of which is three times as powerful as the Hiroshima bomb. Thirty-one Poseidons patrol the seas at all times. With the bombs on these submarines alone, the Soviet Union could be decimated. Of the remaining 50 percent, an approximately equal number are deployed on Minuteman III land-based missiles and B-52 airplanes.

Nearly 75 percent of Soviet bombs are on land-based missiles, a decided disadvantage because the land-based leg of the nuclear triad is the most vulnerable to enemy attack. The vulnerability of these Soviet weapons is further increased by the fact that many are fueled by liquid. These liquid-fueled weapons take longer to launch and are less reliable than the solid-fueled American weapons. Soviet submarines are also less advanced, smaller and easier to track than American submarines. Because they require more frequent fueling and servicing, they spend more time in bases than American submarines and are thus more vulnerable to attack.[6]

THE MILITARY BUILD-UP IN
THE 1980S

In spite of enormous overkill capabilities, during the 1980s the United States engaged in the most extensive and expensive military build-up in its peacetime history. The last budget submitted by President Carter, shortly before he left office in 1980, called for defense expenditures of $160 billion. That figure was nearly doubled by the end of the decade. In the first trillion-dollar budget ever, submitted to Congress by President Reagan for fiscal year 1988, the president requested defense expenditures of $312 billion.[7] Defense spending greatly exceeds federal spending in other areas. For example, in fiscal year 1986, 54 percent of each tax dollar was spent on defense, compared to 7 percent on health, 2.5 percent on education, 2.5 percent on food and nutrition and only 2 percent on housing.[8]

An important part of the military build-up of the 1980s was an increase in the number of nuclear bombs. The production of nuclear bombs was increased by 64 percent, although this cost is not reflected in the defense budget because the bombs are paid for out of the Energy Department's budget. Between 1980 and 1990 approximately 17,000 new bombs were produced. In addition the replacement of all three legs of the nuclear delivery system began. B-52 bombers are being replaced by the B-1 bomber, which in turn will be replaced by the Stealth bomber; land-based Minuteman III missiles are being replaced by the MX missile; and Poseidon submarines are being replaced by Trident submarines armed with the new Trident I missile, soon to be replaced by the newer and more accurate Trident II.

The Trident submarine is the most lethal weapon in history. Every Trident can carry 408 nuclear weapons, each five times as powerful as the Hiroshima bomb. The government plans to build fourteen of these at a cost of $1.5 billion to $2 billion each. Eventually, as many as forty Trident submarines may be built. It is hard to understand the rationale for such numbers of these weapons, since there are only 218 cities in the Soviet Union with a population of 100,000 or more. A single Trident submarine could deliver the equivalent of more than nine Hiroshima-size bombs to each of these cities.

In addition to the replacement of the land-, sea- and air-based delivery systems, the United States is deploying a new weapons system, the cruise missile system, plans for which were laid during the Carter administration. Cruise missiles are small, automated airplanes that carry one nuclear bomb each. They are "smart" missiles, with a computer programmed with a course to the target and a map of the area over which they will fly. This, together with their infrared eye for scanning, allows them to fly over mountains and beneath radar and to zoom in with absolute accuracy on the designated target. Cruise missiles can be launched from ground, sea or air.

All these weapons systems have one thing in common: they are "first-strike weapons." That is, they have the absolute accuracy required to seek out and destroy unlaunched enemy weapons, which must be hit directly to be destroyed because they are underground and protected by thick layers of concrete. Such weapons do not deter attack by threatening a devastating retaliation on enemy cities and industries but are offensive weapons intended to destroy enemy weapons before they have been launched. According to some strategists, such first-strike weapons create instability by making each side nervous about the security of its own weapons systems and may thus encourage a government to launch weapons if it merely believes itself to be under attack. The cruise missile presents an additional problem in that its small size makes detection difficult. This jeopardizes the arms control process because arms control agreements have been possible only when each side is convinced it can detect the other's violations.

NUCLEAR WAR: A PRIMER

Nuclear weapons kill by blast, fire and radiation. While the first two were anticipated, death by radiation poisoning was unknown and unanticipated at the dawn of the nuclear age. Scientists at first did not understand the phenomenon of radiation sickness. After the bombings of Hiroshima and Nagasaki, Japanese doctors thought radiation sickness was an epidemic of a new infectious disease.[9]

A nuclear blast first produces heat of ten million degrees Celsius or more, over three hundred times as much as a chemical explosion. This enormous heat vaporizes everything at close range and creates firestorms hot enough to melt both glass and metal. The blast effect is produced by a high-density, high-temperature ball of gas at the center of the explosion. This gas expands rapidly, producing shock waves and high winds that sweep away from the point of impact.[10] This creates a vacuum into which winds from the surrounding area rush back at speeds at times in excess of five hundred miles per hour, sweeping everyone and everything in their path away.

Victims of blast and heat would die immediately. Many of those afflicted with radiation sickness, however, would not be so fortunate but would linger in agony for days or even weeks before death.[11] Medical personnel attempting to treat victims of radiation would be unable to distinguish those who had received fatal doses of radiation and would die despite treatment from those who might be saved with the proper treatment.[12]

Environmental damage of incalculable extent is also inevitable in the event of a large-scale nuclear war. The National Academy of Sciences reported that a war using half of the strategic weapons held by the United States and the Soviet Union would reduce the ozone layer in the northern hemisphere by 30 to 70 percent. This would result in the destruction of many plants and animals and a dramatic increase in the number of skin cancers among humans.[13] In addition, according to Dr. Kosta Tsipis, professor of physics at Massachusetts Institute of Technology, "All visual organisms—insects, birds, and mammals—would be blinded" if they ventured outside.[14] The widespread destruction of forests, soil and plant life in the event of a major nuclear exchange would result in severe famine—if any human beings remained alive to experience famine. In addition, radioactive pollution would contaminate all plant life and water sources, making them unsafe for consumption.

The destruction of public sanitation facilities and the presence of millions of unburied, decomposing animal and human corpses would provide optimum breeding conditions for rats and insects, much more resistant to radiation than human beings. As a result, epidemics of unprecedented proportions could be expected.

Since medical personnel and equipment tend to be concentrated in the areas likely to be nearest the blast centers, survivors of an attack could expect little medical attention—even just to alleviate pain.

A more recently identified effect of nuclear war is the "nuclear winter effect." A large-scale nuclear attack would lift so much dust and debris into the stratosphere that sunlight would be blotted out for as long as six months. There would be darkness over the whole earth, and temperatures everywhere would fall below freezing for months, destroying food sources and further reducing the chances for survival.

The bottom line in any estimate of the effects of nuclear war is death. The official report of the United States Office of Technology Assessment estimates that up to 190 million Americans, or 86 percent of the population, would die.[15]

The frightening effects of nuclear war are obvious to those who study the subject. In recent years, however, social scientists have begun pointing out the psychological impact of the arms race—namely, that the continued accumulation of nuclear weapons, the nations' increasing reliance on them for security, and the escalating defense expenditures that the arms race entails are in themselves undermining the health of society and the human psyche and putting the future of the human species in jeopardy.

THE ECONOMICS OF THE ARMS RACE

Since World War II, many politicians and economists have suggested that large military expenditures are good for the economy because they create jobs and therefore prosperity. In recent years, however, studies by scholars such as Seymour Melman and Lloyd J. Dimas have questioned this assumption. Research has led many to conclude that while a high level of military spending might create short-term economic prosperity, in the long run it undermines the health of the economy. And, it is argued, even in the short run, military spending is an expensive and inefficient way to create prosperity.

The Civilian Economy

Economist Seymour Melman has argued that high military spending over a long period results in the concentration of scientific and economic resources in the military sector and the consequent neglect of the civilian economy.[16] In recent years, for example, between one-third and one-half of all American research scholars have worked on military projects. These researchers tend to be the best in the field, since salaries are generally higher in the military sector of the economy than in the civilian sector. Since World War II, 60 percent of all government research and development money has been invested in the military. One result of this concentration of economic and scientific resources in the military sector is that while military technology continues to advance, civilian technologies stagnate or advance at a much slower rate. American steel and auto manufacturing and electronic technologies, for example, have become outmoded because so many human and material resources have been devoted to military research.

The opposite is true in Germany and Japan, where research and money are devoted to the improvement of civilian technologies. Constraints placed on Germany and Japan after World War II restrained these nations' military development. This is one of the reasons they have invested less in military research and development and more in the development of the civilian economy. The result is that they have a competitive advantage over the United States in consumer products. The other superpower, the Soviet Union, is in a similar though worse position than the United States. It, too, has given priority to the military sector and is in a poor competitive position over against other nations when it comes to consumer goods.

Melman further disputes the popular belief that the overall effect of high military spending is to create jobs.[17] It cannot be denied, of course, that the production of weapons and other war-related goods produces jobs. Studies, including those by Melman, David Gold and Lloyd Dimas, have indicated, however, that military spending is among the least efficient ways to create jobs.[18] For example, a government investment of $1 billion would create 29,402 jobs in missile production. The same amount would create 45,397 jobs in mass transportation, 38,650 in solar energy and conservation, or 38,192 in public utilities. For the military industry in general, 45,000 jobs are created per $1 billion spent, as compared with 72,000 jobs for police, 76,000 for teachers, or 85,000 for nurses.[19] If, as in recent years, increased military spending is in part financed by the reduction or elimination of government support for other, more labor-intensive programs, increased military spending could result in the loss of jobs.

The practical discussion of the economic effects of high military spending, of course, does not take into account the serious moral issues raised by the idea of using weapons production to create jobs.

DEVELOPMENT AND THE ARMS RACE: AT AN IMPASSE

Nuclear weapons and the arms race are already killing millions, even though the weapons are not being used. Arms expenditures consume resources that are desperately needed to support development efforts in the Third World. A United Nations study asserts that the world must choose between development and the arms race because the resources, both human and financial, are not available for both.[20] Without development there can be no significant progress toward eliminating such fundamental problems as malnutrition, disease, high infant mortality, reduced life span, lack of education and others described in chapter 2.

The superpowers' obsession with armaments is related in another way to the struggle of the poorer countries and peoples for justice. Ultimately it is their weapons systems that enable the superpowers to control the global community and maintain the existing power relationships, both within Third World nations and between these nations and themselves. We have already seen, for example, how the United States has intervened to destabilize and overthrow Third World governments that adopt economic or political policies not to its liking. The Soviet Union has practiced the same sort of interference. The threat of covert or overt intervention by superpowers in the affairs of Third World nations ultimately is backed up by the nuclear arsenals of the United States and the Soviet Union.

Pope Paul VI expressed this integral relationship between the arms race and development when he said, "The new name for peace is development."[21] Without peace there can be no development, and without development there can be no true peace.

PSYCHOLOGICAL DIMENSIONS OF
THE ARMS RACE

In a 1981 Gallup poll, a majority of Americans feared that the United States would be involved in a nuclear war with the Soviet Union. Of this majority, 91 percent believed that such a war could not be limited, 68 percent believed that chances of the war in the next ten years were great, and 68 percent thought that they wouldn't survive. Only 18 percent, however, thought or worried much about it.[22] This is an example of what psychologists such as Robert Lifton call "psychic numbing," and it is one of the main obstacles to massive, effective political mobilization to end the arms race. People are so overwhelmed by the magnitude of the problem and so convinced of their own helplessness that they numb themselves to the nuclear danger.

The existence of the bomb and the apparently uncontrollable dynamic of the arms race have had other effects on the collective psyche as well. Melanie Morris, a United Church of Christ pastor, reports on a series of interviews she conducted with young people thirteen to fifteen years old. She asked them what they expected to be doing in the year 2000. Their answers were so depressing that in transcribing them she had to stop the tape every few minutes because she was crying too hard to go on. This thirteen-year-old's response was typical: "I don't think much about the future. With everything going on in the world, someone might push the button. Sometimes I think I'd like to do something, but then I think, there won't be a future. I don't get my hopes up too high."[23]

Professor Edwin S. Schneidman has researched the effects of the bomb on the human psyche. In his classes at Harvard and the University of California at Los Angeles on death and dying, he questioned students who had grown up in the post-Hiroshima age about their psychic experiences. The comment of this twenty-one-year-old student is typical:

> I'm sure a week doesn't go by when I don't seriously consider the possibility of nuclear catastrophe. . . . I used as a child to be struck dumb with the thought of being killed by an atomic bomb, but as I grew I realized that if I remained in cities like New York, Boston or London, I would hardly have time to realize I was going to be dead before I would be.[24]

Michael Mandelbaum, associate professor of government at Harvard, reports a similar conversation with a student of his who said,

> I do not drink, take drugs, sleep around, live chaotically, believe in revolutionary politics, gamble, and avoid planning solely because of the existence of the threat, but I certainly would be willing to wager it has something to do with it, since its images are inescapable in daily life.[25]

Reflecting on these and innumerable other cases of psychological disorientation and behavioral aberration occasioned at least in part by the bomb, many observers have drawn some dark conclusions. Sociologist Christopher Lasch, in *The Culture of Narcissism*, says, "Impending disaster has become an everyday concern, so commonplace and familiar that nobody any longer gives much thought to how it can be averted."[26] Robert Lifton, in *The Broken Connection*, declares, "The image of total destruction . . . enters into every relationship involving parents, children and grandparents."[27] William Faulkner, in his acceptance speech for the Nobel Prize in literature in 1950, said, "There are no longer questions of the spirit. There is only the question, 'when will I be blown up?'"[28] T. S. Eliot, in his *Twentieth Century Book of the Dead*, writes, "Since the atom bomb and its successors in death technology, the new possibility of total death for the species has become a reality."[29]

Diagnosing the age on the basis of his examination, Schneidman concludes,

> The psychological fallout from yet unexploded bombs has created a chronic low-grade psychic infection throughout the world. . . . Our age is characterized by a pervasive thanatological aura traceable to an evil that is visibly personified and made assailable in the omnipresent threat of nuclear destruction.[30]

Schneidman expresses in religious terms the challenge with which the nuclear reality confronts us:

> We are at a fulcrum time in the psychological history of man, vibrating in mid-deep, debating . . . whether to sink into "the speechless profound of the sea" or to bound up into the blessed air, whether to respond to the imperious call to life or to succumb to the constant invitation that death seductively puts forth.[31]

DOING THEOLOGY IN THE
NUCLEAR AGE

These comments on the nuclear crisis, like my previous remarks on the economic crisis, are not theology in the traditional sense. They are rather a secular introduction or prolegomenon to theology, an attempt to follow Jesus' advice to become as wise as serpents about the world in which we live by describing important characteristics of it. This is the world, after all, within which and for which we must theologize. To do this, we must know the world and love it. Nuclear annihilation is a unique and perhaps the most overwhelming threat to the world, and therefore we must face up to it.

Albert Einstein, whose theory of relativity provided the theoretical basis for the development of nuclear technology, wrote, "As scientists, we dare not slacken in our efforts to make the people of the world, and especially their governments, aware of the unspeakable disaster they are certain to provoke unless they change their attitudes toward one another and recognize their responsibility in shaping a safe future."[32] Evolution teaches us that only those species capable of adapting to changes in their environment survive. Einstein suggests that the advent of nuclear weapons represents an environmental change so drastic that it demands a radical adaptation in human behavior. The adaptation required is the elimination of war and of those conditions that have made recourse to war as a means of resolving international conflict inevitable. Foremost among these conditions is the absence of global authority structures that would make war both unnecessary and impossible. Unless our species can accomplish this adaptation, it is likely in the near future to become extinct on planet earth.

Indeed, in light of developments since Einstein's time, we can go even further and say that more than a change in thinking is required. What is required is a radical change in the way we perceive the world and our relationship to it. We must learn to see the world as one undivided reality rather than as separate pieces pitted against each other in a struggle for survival. We must learn to see the choice before us as a choice between *one* world and *no* world. When we learn to perceive reality in this way, the counterproductive nature of reliance on weapons of mass destruction will become obvious, and our political values and behaviors will change, as they must if we are to survive the crisis before which we stand.

Unfortunately, such a radical perceptual and behavioral change, which in Christian tradition is called *conversion*, is not easily achieved. To bring about such change, however, is precisely the object of the church's evangelistic mission to the world. Authentic evangelism seeks to connect people to the gospel vision of an undivided world and to mobilize them to work for the realization of that vision by the overcoming of every form of alienation and enmity through the love of God revealed and released in the world in Jesus.

Such conversion is a sure cure for the idolatry and nihilism that leads so many today to rely on the power of weapons and wealth for their security. Conversion to the gospel vision is certain to affect not only the behavior of individuals but the social and political life of nations and the international community. In Part Two I will explore the nature of this vision so that we may discover how and why this is so.

PART TWO

THE TRIUNE GOD AND THE QUEST FOR JUSTICE AND PEACE

4

GOD AND
ISRAEL

In the following chapters I reflect theologically in a way that confronts the serious world problems that I have described in Part One. I do not attempt to respond to these problems point by point but allow them to provide the context within which the following reflections occur. This context influences profoundly the perspective from which we approach the Christian faith tradition, the questions that we ask that tradition and the perceptions and conclusions that we draw from it.

This approach to theology does not presuppose that our understanding of Christian faith and life can be derived from our knowledge of the world or our experience in it. Rather, it acknowledges its dependence on the revelation of God as recorded in Scripture and interpreted by the faith community throughout the ages. What distinguishes it from a more historicist or dogmatic approach and certainly from a fundamentalist one is its assertion that our understanding of God's self-revelation and its implications for our life in the world are influenced by our experiences as Christians living in the midst of the crises of our own society and time. To bring these two realities—Christian faith and history—into fruitful relationship is precisely the job of theology.

This assertion confronts us with a dilemma. On the one hand, we must seek to be faithful to the unique nature of God's revelation. This means respect for the traditional sources of theology— Scripture and the interpretive tradition of the church, especially the doctrinal tradition. On the other hand, we must seek to be faithful to our own experience as modern men and women who participate in various histories and cultures. We must risk undertaking creative interpretations and reinterpretations of God's revelation that are informed by and relevant to our own experience. Although such undertakings expose us to the danger of heresy, to turn away from them inevitably results in irrelevance, which is itself a form of heresy because it does not take the doctrine of the incarnation seriously. As we give ourselves to this work of reinterpretation, we must rely on the Holy Spirit to keep us faithful and to lead us beyond the realm of merely cognitive knowledge *about* God into the realm of personal knowledge *of* God and God's will. Such knowledge comes from a relationship with God and participation, through Christ and the Spirit, in the life of God.

The Orthodox tradition expresses the posture appropriate for the theologian longing to know God in this way: "Center the mind in the heart." As one Orthodox theologian puts it, "Those who want to establish the one thought of God within themselves, are advised to leave the head and descend *with their mind* into their heart, and to stand there with ever present attention."[1] This understanding of the relationship between head and heart is not anti-intellectual but integrative. The mind is engaged (descend *with the mind*), but the mind is united with the heart. Intellect, emotion, passion, understanding and will all must be engaged in an integrative fashion in the theological undertaking. In other words, prayer, as an expression of our living relationship with God, is as essential to the theological task as intellectual training in theological methodologies, Scripture or the doctrinal tradition. Karl Barth expresses this role of prayer in theology in a book on Anselm, which he considered to be one of his most important—*Fides Quarens Itellectum*. Barth emphasizes that for Anselm the knowledge of God that provides the basis for proving God's existence "must be sought in prayer."[2] This insight into the relationship between prayer and theology also undergirds Barth's own work in *Church Dogmatics*.

Anselm's and Barth's early writings were monologues, conversations with oneself *about* God; their later writings were dialogues *with* God. Such dialogues are grounded in prayer, that is, in relationship with God.

This understanding of the theological task is also found in the writings of Flemish mystic Jan van Ruysbroek:

> That is the highest recognition of God which man can have in the active life; that he should recognize in the light of faith that God is beyond comprehension and cognition. In this light Christ says to man's desire: "Go down quickly because today I dwell in your house." This hasty going down is nothing else but the soul's flowing down with desire and love into the depths of the Godhead which no understanding can touch in created light. But desire and love go in where understanding is not admitted. When the soul thus inclines herself with love with intent towards God *beyond* that which she understands, then in this she rests and dwells in God and God in her.[3]

Without some experience of friendship and intimacy with God, expressed in mystical language by van Ruysbroek, Christian theology, teaching and preaching are only hearsay. Such hearsay may be passed on for centuries in the form of stock theological phrases or even doctrines, but it will lack power, authority and credibility because it is not based on experience of God and God's love. Therefore, in order to speak about God and God's gospel, we must also speak with God and God with us. We must seek to live with and in God. These are the concerns of spirituality.[4]

In the following chapters I reflect on certain questions that I consider fundamental to Christian faith, attempting to employ the theological methodology I have outlined. These questions are: (1) Who is Jesus Christ for us today and what light does he shed on our total life experience in the world? (2) What light does Jesus Christ shed on our understanding of God, the world and ourselves? (3) How do these new understandings to which Jesus leads us transform our relationships, attitudes, priorities, commitments and engagements in the world? (4) In light of our reflections on the above questions and of the knowledge of our world gained from Part One, what might we conclude about our calling as Christian people and about the mission of the church in today's world?[5]

THE SCRIPTURAL COMMUNITY'S
UNDERSTANDING OF GOD

The theology of peace and justice in the following chapters rests on the Christian doctrine of God as I understand it. I believe that a vision based on fundamental Christian doctrine provides a more secure foundation for a theology of peace and justice than what I would call a biblical positivism. By biblical positivism, I mean an approach that takes specific biblical passages and seeks to draw very specific and sometimes legalistic political, economic and ethical conclusions from them in a proof-testing manner.[6]

I have chosen the Christian understanding of God as the foundation for a theology of peace and justice because I believe that all other dimensions of a faith-informed vision, including our understanding of the *shalom* that is God's will and gift for all creation, should flow from our understanding of God. This understanding of God has emerged over time from experiences of the believing community that were understood as experiences of God. These experiences were passed on to future generations through liturgical celebrations and oral recitations and finally were recorded in the Scriptures. These oral and written accounts preserve the memory of these experiences, the community's interpretation(s) of them and the conclusions about God and God's will for the world that these experiences and interpretations led to. Figure 1 is a diagram of the complicated relationship between human experience, Christian experience, revelatory events, the scriptural record and later interpretations of these events and the conclusions about God and God's will the community of believers was led to as it celebrated and contemplated these events.

The experiences of the faith community recorded in Scripture are historical; they occurred over a period of nearly two thousand years. Likewise, the conclusions about God drawn from these experiences have a history in which the community's understanding of God evolved. For example, the understanding of God in Second Isaiah is not the same as that in Judges and the understanding in Ruth is not the same as that in Ezra or Nahum. Though there is probably a chronological element in the development of the biblical community's understanding of God, different, even

FIGURE 1

contradictory, understandings of God often appear concurrently. Perhaps there were several understandings of God in the biblical community, each of which underwent its own evolution. Certainly there seems to be one tradition that understands God in narrower, more nationalistic terms and another that understands God in more universalistic terms. Some understandings appear to put greater emphasis on the severity of God's judgment, others on the overwhelming grace and mercy of God.

In the following chapters I seek to illumine the experience of the faith community out of which the Christian understanding of God developed.

THE BIBLICAL GOD OF JUSTICE

The Exodus

Perhaps the best way to begin talking about the biblical God is to consider the exodus event. The exodus is seen by many Christian and Jewish scholars as the central event through which God is revealed in the Old Testament. Jewish scholar Henry Englander writes, "The Exodus, when judged by the influence which the memory of it exercised in biblical and rabbinic times, stands forth as one of the supreme facts and periods in our history."[7] The most convincing support for Englander's assertion is found in the Old Testament itself—the Torah, the Psalms, the Prophets and the history books are replete with references and allusions to the exodus. In fact, outside the exodus narratives themselves, Englander lists over 140 references to the exodus in the Old Testament.[8] For example, in Deuteronomy, "The Sabbath is enjoined for all as a memorial of Egyptian slavery. The emancipation which made Israel a free people was . . . made the ground for the prohibition against holding a . . . Hebrew in permanent bondage. The oft repeated refrain, 'remember that ye were slaves in Egypt' practically calls for self-identification on the part of each generation with those who suffered in actual slavery."[9] Prophets such as Amos and Second Isaiah also refer to the exodus as a paradigmatic event that revealed God's will for Israel and for the world. Indeed, the exodus was so central to Israel's understanding of God that God is sometimes identified simply as "the God of the exodus."

What does the exodus event tell us about God? An increasing number of biblical scholars and theologians insist that the exodus reveals Yahweh as a God who is allied not with the rulers of society but with the poor and oppressed.[10] Yahweh is the God whose ears and heart are open to the cries of the oppressed and who intervenes in their behalf. Yahweh puts the mighty down from their thrones and exalts the lowly, sends the rich away empty and fills the hungry with good things. Yahweh does not legitimize existing property or power relationships or sanctify the social status quo but overthrows unjust social orders and liberates the oppressed. Walter Brueggemann expresses the difference between Yahweh and the gods of Egypt this way: Yahweh steps into the brickyard and says, "Let my people go!" whereas the gods of Egypt say, "Make more bricks."[11] According to Jean Cardonnel, "The specific character of the one and only God is the fact that he intervenes in the very midst of abandonment and dereliction. His divine revelation begins with the liberation of the most oppressed and tortured people who thereby move prophetically from oppression to liberation."[12]

There are, of course, those who disagree with this interpretation and theology of the exodus. French theologian François Biot, for example, maintains that the interpretation of the exodus as an event revealing God as liberator of the oppressed is acceptable as a personal preference but that the Bible itself does not interpret the exodus this way. Biot further maintains that even if the Bible did interpret the exodus as an event of political liberation of the oppressed and thus reveal God as liberator, this would not hallow or legitimate revolution, because political and ethical norms cannot be derived from biblical stories.[13]

Responding to this criticism, Spanish theologian Alfredo Fierro points out that the exegetical question of how the exodus is to be interpreted has not yet been settled. Admitting that proponents of the liberation perspective may too hastily assume that the exodus is an act of resistance, insurrection and liberation, Fierro believes that Biot is equally hasty in rejecting this interpretation. Fierro's suggestion is that we let the exegetes decide this question. Moreover, Fierro insists that the liberationist understanding of the exodus is not ultimately dependent on the biblical *interpretation* of the exodus since the story itself, as told by the biblical narrator, clearly describes an act of political liberation.[14]

It seems to me, however, that there is much in the Bible that supports a liberationist understanding of the exodus. That the prophets interpret the exodus as a liberating event with continuing significance for the life of Israel is clear from their appeal to the exodus in support of their own demands for social justice. Amos, for example, continually alludes to the exodus, claiming that Israel has become like Egypt because of the injustice and oppression in its midst. He warns that Yahweh will act again to put an end to this oppression. Surely Amos's use of the exodus supports a liberationist interpretation of this event. Second Isaiah's reference to the exodus as a prototype for a second act of deliverance, this time from Babylonian captivity, also supports the interpretation of the exodus as an act of political liberation.

Fierro admits that the exodus story, however interpreted, obligates no one to engage in revolution. He insists, however, that the exodus, like all other major events of so-called salvation history, functions as an archetype or paradigm. If these cardinal events of salvation history had no value for Christians as exemplars or prototypes, they would have no importance at all. As an archetype portraying God and the Israelite forebears as participants in a revolutionary act of liberation, the biblical narrative of the exodus *authorizes* people of faith to participate, under certain circumstances, in revolutionary struggles to liberate themselves and to do so on the basis of their faith and belief that God calls them to the struggle and struggles with them. In other words, "The biblical narrative of the escape from Egypt liberates people from the fear of revolution."[15] It frees them to disobey political authority and certifies that insurrection is a possible line of action for people who believe in the God of the exodus.

The Law: The Institutionalization
of Liberation

In the theology of the Torah, the exodus event through which God is revealed as powerful liberator of Israel issues immediately in the call to be a covenant community and to live a covenant life. At Sinai and during the long wandering in the wilderness, this community and its life begin to take shape. Definitive for the shape of the community's life is trust in the covenant faithfulness (*hesed*) of Yahweh revealed in the exodus. At the Red Sea, at Sinai and in the wilderness, Israel had no army, no national treasury, no king or nobles in which to trust; Israel had no alternative but to trust in Yahweh. It was Yahweh's providence alone that made survival in the desert possible.

The Ten Commandments begin, "I am the Lord your God, who brought you out of the land of Egypt, out of the house of bondage. You shall have no other gods before me. You shall not make for yourself a graven image. . . . You shall not take the name of the Lord your God in vain" (Exod. 20:2-4, 7). In other words, trust in the *hesed* of God alone and do not seek to use God for your own purposes; do not seek to gain power *over* God. This introduction is followed by seven commandments that order the life of the community. Faithfulness to these commandments is Israel's *response* to the exodus. Fulfillment of this covenant stands as a concrete sign of Israel's trust in Yahweh and an expression of its gratitude for being delivered. By regulating its life on the basis of these laws, Israel becomes a just society—an alternative to Egypt—and preserves and institutionalizes the gift of liberation received through the exodus. Thus distinguished from other nations, Israel fulfills its vocation in the world as an ensign pointing to the true God, the God of the exodus, of covenant faithfulness, and of justice.[16]

In other words. the Pentateuch connects the proclamation of God's liberation through the exodus with the call to respond to this liberation by trusting in God alone and faithfully observing those obligations of covenant life that ensure social justice and therefore continue the benefits of the exodus in the life of the covenant community. This response is Israel's vocation in the world, a part of its evangelistic mission.

In addition to the Ten Commandments, other laws in the Pentateuch are closely connected with the exodus and Israel's understanding of God as liberator of the oppressed. Such laws are found in the Covenant Code (Exod. 20:22-23), the Holiness Code (Lev. 17—26) and Deuteronomy, and include the gleaning law, the Sabbath year law, the jubilee year law, laws protecting strangers, widows and orphans and the law prohibiting interest on loans, all of which give concrete expression to the covenant life.

The gleaning law (Lev. 19:9-10; 23:22; Deut. 24:19-21) regulates harvesting practice. Those who own fields in Israel are not to harvest the fields to their borders or go over the fields a second time. They are not to pick up the grapes that fall to the ground or strip their vineyards or olive trees bare. The grain at the borders of the fields and the gleanings after the harvest as well as the unharvested and fallen grapes and olives belong to the poor.

The Sabbath year law (Exod. 23:22; Deut. 15:1-18) requires that every seventh year all fields be allowed to lie fallow, all Israelite slaves be freed and the debts of all fellow Israelites be cancelled. During that year, whatever grows on the fields, vines and trees is for the poor and the wild beasts. Deuteronomy requires that the freed slaves be provided with livestock, grain and wine. The rationale for this custom of freeing Hebrew slaves is God's act of freeing Israel from slavery in Egypt.

A jubilee year is to be observed every forty-nine or fifty years. The jubilee year legislation (Lev. 25:8-55) prescribes the same measures as those for the Sabbath year. In addition, property is to be returned to its original owners.

Other passages forbid the charging of interest on loans of money or goods to a fellow Israelite (Exod. 22:25; Lev. 25:36-37; Deut. 23:19-20) and invoke the community to protect and care for the widow, the fatherless and the sojourner (Deut. 10:18-19). These ethical exhortations are theologically grounded in Israel's experience of God in the exodus and on the understanding of God to which that experience led. The Lord "executes justice for the fatherless and the widow, and loves the sojourner, giving him food and clothing. Love the sojourner therefore; for you were sojourners in the land of Egypt" (Deut. 10:18-19).

These laws concerning land management and economics are based upon fundamental theological presuppositions held by the prophetic community of Israel, including the following: (1) God is the Lord of the nation and sovereign over all dimensions of its life; (2) God wants to create a community truly different from Egypt—a community whose institutions reflect its faith in the God of the exodus by serving the causes of justice, community solidarity and freedom; (3) economic life is particularly significant in any attempt to institutionalize and prolong the exodus experience of liberation in the life of the community; (4) God is the owner of all things, including the land, and insists that property be managed in a way that promotes economic justice and equality; (5) as owner, God issues specific and concrete rules that regulate the economic affairs of the community, and the human managers of God's property are expected to observe these rules conscientiously; (6) these rules serve the cause of economic justice by prohibiting the accumulation of wealth or property by individuals or families, thereby ensuring a reasonably just distribution of goods. This belief that God is the sole owner of society's property and wealth and is committed to economic justice conflicts with modern capitalism's veneration of private property and belief in the right of people to accumulate as much as they can and use it in any way they see fit. Indeed, the beliefs and values of classical laissez-faire economic philosophy are about as far from biblical beliefs and values as they could be.

The prophets realized that economic greed is one of the most powerful temptations for individuals, classes and societies, as their many denunciations of economic injustice reveal. In their efforts to structure the life of the community according to the canons of God's justice, these laws reflect the influence of this prophetic realization by the special attention they pay to the economic life of the covenant community. They seek to protect individuals and groups against their own and others' greed.

Underlying this concern for economic justice are two profound religious issues. The first is the primary religious issue in Israel—idolatry. Wealth has always been one of the most common idols. The prophets of Israel sought to create safeguards against the idolatrous worship and service of wealth by forbidding efforts to accumulate wealth, warning of the spiritual dangers connected with its accumulation and erecting obstacles to accumulation.

The second religious issue underlying the biblical focus on economics is one of mission. Israel is to be a light to the nations by bearing witness to the God of the exodus—the liberator God who hears the cries of the oppressed and delivers them from their oppressors. This task requires Israel to embody the gift of liberation in its social life by protecting and respecting the weak and the poor. The prophets were wise enough to recognize that exhortations to charity were not enough to accomplish this task. Social legislation designed to restrain the greed of the mighty and ensure the well-being of the weak was also necessary. If Israel ignored this task it would become like Egypt and the credibility of its witness to the God of the exodus would be undermined.

The Prophets: The Restoration of Identity and Mission

The prophets react to what they see as Israel's unfaithfulness to its identity and mission. Israel's identity is a function of its trusting relationship to Yahweh. Israel's mission is to bear witness to

Yahweh in word and in deed. This implies taking seriously God's call to be a liberated society. The prophets accuse Israel of the fundamental sins of idolatry and injustice, that is, of failure to trust in Yahweh alone and to practice justice. Because of the biblical understanding of God as the God of the exodus, these two sins are integrally related throughout the Bible.[17] For the prophets, in fact, injustice is itself a form of idolatry because it reveals ignorance of the true God. As José P. Miranda says, "To know Yahweh" is to "achieve justice for the poor."[18]

In the well-known and powerful passage from chapter 5, the prophet Amos makes the connection between worship and justice:

> I reject your oblations and refuse to look at your sacrifice of
>   fattened cattle
> Let me have no more of the din of your chanting
> No more of your strumming on harps
> But let justice flow like water
> And integrity like an unfailing stream.
>   (Amos 5:21-24, Jerusalem Bible)

This relationship between idolatry and injustice is also expressed in, for example, Isa. 1:11-17; 58:1-12; and Jer. 22:13-16.

The prophets reinforce and intensify Israel's exodus-based understanding of God as liberator and proponent of justice and its understanding of its own missionary vocation to bear witness to this God by being a just and liberated community.

THE BIBLICAL GOD OF PEACE

The understanding of God as liberator of the oppressed led to the assertion that the service God desires from the people of God is that they trust only in God and take great care to see that the injustices of Egypt are not repeated in their midst. But what of my other concern in this book—peace? Does Israel's understanding of God, reflected in the Old Testament, lead also to a passion for peace? The biblical tradition is much more complicated on the matter of violence than on that of justice. A dominant Old Testament image of Yahweh is as a warrior leading Israel into battle against its pagan foes. Furthermore, Yahweh's wars are often portrayed as extraordinarily violent, even genocidal, a fact that offends the consciences of many sensitive people.

Yahweh as Warrior

The biblical portrayal of Yahweh as warrior is entirely compatible with the biblical emphasis on Yahweh as God of justice, but it presents problems for a biblically based theology of peace. Although there is no way to harmonize completely the image of Yahweh as warrior with a theology of peace, I believe a more detailed study of this biblical image reveals that this incongruity is not as absolute as might at first be thought.

Millard C. Lind, in his book *Yahweh Is a Warrior*, points out that to understand the Old Testament's theology of war it is important to realize that Yahweh is seen as the *only* warrior in Israel. Israel's responsibility in the event of war is not to produce warriors and a war machine but to rely *solely* on Yahweh. According to Lind, this unique theology of war has its origin in the experience of the exodus.

> The uniqueness of the Exodus material . . . is that the Hebrew clans were not called to do battle in the usual sense of the word, but to respond to and trust Yahweh as the sole warrior against the military might of Egypt. The Hebrew freedom movement experienced Yahweh as the *sole* bearer of a unique political power and authority addressed both to themselves and their enemy through a prophetic personality. In the human arena the leadership of the warrior was replaced by the leadership of the prophet, one who spoke the word of Yahweh both to the Hebrews and to Egypt. This unique experience of deliverance from Egypt by a prophetic personality rather than by a warrior hero was not an ephemeral event, but was the foundation for a new type of theo-political order, the Kingship of Yahweh.[19]

If Lind is correct, then the prophetic vision of a new type of theo-political order inspired by the exodus experience explains the persistent resistance in Israel, especially in prophetic circles, to the institution of the monarchy. A human king on Israel's throne violates the prophetic confession "Yahweh Melek Israel" ("Yahweh is King of Israel"). This prophetic theo-political vision also explains the origins of the Holy War theory, according to which war, as the ultimate instrument of power, is available to Yahweh alone and is never permitted to human authorities. Even preparations for war by a king or state—creating a standing army, establishing a military hierarchy and an arsenal of weapons, engaging in entangling political alliances with other nations—are considered usurpations of Yahweh's power and represent idolatrous trust in human strength and wisdom rather than in the covenant faithfulness of Yahweh.

According to Lind, this new theo-political vision, of which the Holy War doctrine is an expression,

> created within Israel a fundamental tension between the way of Yahweh and the way of the nations. It was caused . . . by an event within the war tradition itself, that is the deliverance from Egypt. This peculiar way in which mythic experience was mediated to history, through prophecy and miracle, contrasted sharply with the way of warfare and kingship as known among nations. The testimony to this event, inserted into the covenant tradition, was seen as Yahweh's foundational act of grace upon which Israel's government was to be based.[20]

From this, it can be seen that Israel's distinctive theology of warfare, according to which "obedience to Yahweh's word and trust in his miracle are alone decisive,"[21] derives directly from Israel's experience of deliverance at the exodus and leads directly to the understanding of Yahweh as the only warrior in Israel, and to its corollary, the theory of Holy War.

Lind concludes that the prophets' emphasis on social justice and their rejection of a secular theology of the state and of war are both derived from the prophetic theo-political vision, which in turn rests on the prophets' experience and understanding of God.

> The issue was between a divinity who represented an alliance of economic and religious interests backed by political coercion, and a divinity who represented the moral, social and spiritual values of exodus-Sinai, whose economics consisted of faith in his word of promise and whose politics consisted of obedience to his word.[22]

In light of Lind's study, it appears that the biblical tradition of Yahweh as warrior, far from being a blanket justification of the violence of the state and of war, emphasizes the extraordinary nature of the circumstances under which such violence is politically acceptable. Yahweh alone can authorize such violence, and the human means that Yahweh uses for such authorization is not the official ruler of the state but the charismatic prophet whom Yahweh raises up when and where circumstances require it. The portrayal of Yahweh as warrior, then, as well as the concept of Holy War serve to remove the violent instrument of war from the hands of the state. Therefore, the Holy War tradition is consistent with the side of Yahweh's personality that is consistently emphasized in the biblical tradition. Although Yahweh is a passionate warrior against idolatry and injustice, Yahweh is fundamentally opposed to violence and forbids human authority to make war. That alternate weapon in the fight against injustice is reserved for Yahweh's own hands.

Yahweh as Creator

The biblical God is above all a lover of all creation. This understanding of God as gracious lover and nurturer is also connected with the exodus and the events surrounding it. In Moses' experience at the burning bush, which initiates the action leading to the exodus, Yahweh comes forth as the God who hears the cries of these enslaved people in Egypt, sees their miserable state and is resolved to deliver them from their oppressors. The motivation for the story described in Exodus 3—15 is God's compassion for a suffering people, not God's wrath against Egypt. God begins the exodus action not by inflicting suffering on Egypt but by confronting Pharaoh with the demand that the oppressed be liberated. But Pharaoh hardens his heart against this word of God with which the prophet, Moses, confronts him. In so doing, Pharaoh turns what could also have been a liberating word for him into a word of judgment.[23] The plagues and the drowning of Pharaoh and the Egyptian army are the result of Pharaoh's hard heart. They are not a part of God's plan but are caused by resistance to God's liberating will. The purpose of the story is the deliverance of a powerless and enslaved people and the glorification of the invisible and liberating God of Israel over the very visible and oppressive Egyptian empire and its gods. The destruction of Pharaoh and his army are a by-product of that deliverance.

As the story of the exodus shows, from very early on there was a tension between Israel's experience of God as a warrior for justice on the one hand and as a compassionate, liberating and forgiving nurturer on the other. The emphasis on compassion in the divine personality, found already in the exodus story, continues to grow in importance and reaches its final scriptural development in the New Testament. "God is love" (1 John 4:6) is its most succinct and ultimate expression. We will speak of this New Testament development in detail in later chapters. My point here is that this experience of God as love does not spring up full grown in the New Testament but is the essential quality of Israel's experience of God from the very beginning. It is important to emphasize this to counter the popular impression that the God of the Old Testament is authoritarian and wrathful, a deity who must be placated. In this view, as Terence Fretheim points out, Jesus is portrayed as the one who saves us from this God.[24] Anselm's theory of atonement, which has been so dominant in the theology and piety of the Western church, reinforces this impression. However, the God of the Old Testament is portrayed primarily as merciful savior. God's wrath, though real and powerful, is the shadow cast by God's grace when it meets the resistance of human will.

Israel's experience of God as merciful and forgiving reconciler is expressed in many Old Testament passages, of which the following are examples:

> For his anger is but for a moment, and his favor is for a
>   lifetime.
>
> > (Ps. 30:5; cf. Ps. 85:3)

> For a brief moment I forsook you. . . .
> In overflowing wrath for a moment
> I hid my face from you,
> but with everlasting love
> I will have compassion on you.
> > (Isa. 54:7-8)

> When Israel was a child, I loved him,
> and out of Egypt I called my son. . . .
> It was I who taught Ephraim to walk,
> I took them up in my arms;
> but they did not know that I healed them.
> > (Hos. 11:1-3)

The compassionate God is like a mother who never forsakes her children.

> Can a woman forget her sucking child,
> that she should have no compassion on the son of her womb?
> Even these may forget, yet I will not forget you.
>
> (Isa. 49:15, RSV)

Psalms alone speaks 103 times of God's *hesed* (mercy, loving-kindness, steadfast love). In addition, the Old Testament speaks frequently of God's *hanan* (grace) and love. The *Hastings Dictionary of the Bible* has this to say about Israel's experience of God as love as it is expressed in the Old Testament:

> The unique place which love holds in the Israelite as compared with other religions, is due to its insistence on a reciprocal affection of God and people. Abraham is the friend of God, and love to God is even demanded by him. Moreover, the very word which expresses this love is drawn from a sphere which involves a reciprocity, namely marriage relations and intimate friendship (as between David and Jonathan). But humanity's love to God is not primarily spontaneous. Jahweh has loved humanity first and has provoked its response.[25]

One could say that Yahweh's way is to woo the partner (Israel, the church, the world) into the covenant/marriage relationship rather than to frighten, overwhelm and violate. One of the deepest insights of the Old Testament is its awareness of the suffering that God experiences because of God's loving longing for and wooing of an unfaithful partner.

On the basis of these affirmations, we are justified in speaking of the humanism or philanthropy of the Old Testament God.[26] Although God loves all creation, humanity, as the very image and likeness of God in the world, enjoys a special place. As Gerhard von Rad points out, "That means that the pattern on which [humanity] was fashioned is to be sought outside the sphere of the created."[27]

This experience of God as lover of humanity nourishes the vision of a truly just and nonviolent society expressed so beautifully by prophets such as Isaiah, Micah, Jeremiah, Joel and Zechariah. On the basis of this vision the prophets continue to condemn the social status quo for its idolatry, injustice and violence, awaken hope for an alternative society and encourage the quest to make this alternative a reality.

The Prophetic Critique of
Institutional Violence

The quest for economic justice is a part of the prophetic long-ing for a nonviolent society, since economic exploitation is a form of social violence. Another form of institutional violence con-demned by the prophets is political oppression. Generally, political oppression is directly proportional to the concentration of power in the hands of a ruling elite. In Egypt, for example, the pharaoh, son of god and himself divine, owned all land and all wealth and exercised absolute power over the economic and social life of the nation. He used this power to defeat his enemies, extend the area over which he ruled, and build monuments to the glory of himself and his kingdom. The pyramids, which exemplify the pharaoh's narcissism, also symbolize the oppressive social structure of Egypt. Pharaoh and the nobles and priests sit enthroned at the top of the pyramid, supported by the groaning masses at the base, among them the children of Israel.

The social vision espoused by the prophets and inspired by their experience of Yahweh as a just and loving God condemns a politically oppressive social order. It condemns "human manipula-tion and control of the social and political resources involved in the violent exercise of power."[28] Societies like Egypt rely on such power to survive. For the prophets, the norm for Israel's political and social life is the period of wandering in the desert. There, Israel was required to trust in Yahweh alone, whose presence was symbolized by the ark of the covenant, the mobile throne on which the invisi-ble Yahweh sat. Israel was given not a statue of God but only an empty space in which to trust. Along with the absence of political power in the usual sense, however, was the absence of a ruling class that oppressed the people. Rather, Yahweh, Redeemer God of the exodus, Creator and Nourisher of the covenant community, ruled Israel in justice, love and equity.

"Yahweh Melek Israel" was Israel's religious and political creed. When the monarchy was finally established, a protracted struggle began between prophets and kings that permeated Israel's history from the time of Samuel and Saul through the time of Jeremiah and Zedekiah. The prophets saw an important part of their task to be to remind the king that it was not his duty to aggrandize or enrich himself or the nation. Nor was it primarily his duty to defend the nation against its enemies—that was Yahweh's job. The king was to ensure justice by enforcing the Torah of Yahweh. As Walter Brueggemann puts it, "The task set for the king is surprising and perhaps doubtful. The king is to sit all day on his throne and read the Torah. And Torah, as you know, is talk about *mispat* and *sedeqah*, about justice and righteousness."[29]

As the monarchy developed, however, the power that belonged rightfully to God, including the power to make war, was usurped by the state and the king. Rather than enforce justice, the kings tolerated or even inflicted injustice on the nation and contributed to the "ruin of Joseph" (Amos 6:6). They allowed the accumulation of power and wealth until Israel's social structure began to resemble that of Egypt. Some kings attempted to suppress Yahwehism—in part, perhaps, to escape the condemnation of Yahweh's prophets. These kings preferred other gods who cared little for justice and peace so long as their cult was served and their name honored with the correct religious ceremonies. The history of Israel, as recorded in 1 and 2 Kings and Chronicles and corroborated by the prophets, bears witness to the apostasy of Israel's kings, their usurpation of Yahweh's prerogatives and oppression of their subjects.

Connected with the kings' abuse of their power is the emergence in Israel of the idolatry of the state. The state and its ruler replace God as the object of the people's trust, the power they look to for their security and well-being. Isaiah 31:1 warns of the dire consequences to come of this development:

> Woe to those who go down to Egypt for help
>   and rely on horses,
> who trust in chariots because they are many
> and in horsemen because they are very strong,
> but do not look to the Holy One of Israel
> or consult the Lord![30]

From the prophetic perspective, much violence—the violence of power politics and war, the violence of political and economic oppression and the violence of Yahweh's judgment—would have been avoided if Israel had remained faithful to the covenant principles of trust in Yahweh and the practice of justice. Because Israel refused to be led by God into the ways of truth, justice and nonviolence, it called down upon itself the violent judgment of God expressed in the exile. The significance of this biblical history is not, of course, that Israel is more wicked than other nations. Rather, the preservation of Israel's story reveals God's special relationship with and commitment to Israel. The case of Israel is paradigmatic: it reveals the dynamic operative in the history of all nations and serves as a warning to any nation that persists in the idolatrous illusion of its own omnipotence, tolerates injustice and relies on violence and oppression to secure its future.

The Prophetic Vision of a New Social Order

Understanding Yahweh as the God of steadfast love, the prophets not only criticized and condemned the existing social order but in numerous eschatological passages they poetically imaged an alternative to this order. They viewed this alternative not as a possibility for the future but as a *certainty* because of Yahweh's justice, grace and faithfulness. The poems of the prophet Isaiah regarding the coming age of *shalom* are perhaps the most beautiful expression of this prophetic vision.

> For every boot of the tramping warrior
>   in battle tumult
> and every garment rolled in blood
> will be burned as fuel for the fire.
> For to us a child is born,
>   to us a son is given;
> and the government will be upon his shoulder;
> and his name will be called
> "Wonderful Counselor, Mighty God,
>   Everlasting Father, Prince of Peace."
>   (Isa. 9:5-6)

> The wolf shall dwell with the lamb,
> and the leopard shall lie down with the kid,
> and the calf and the lion and the fatling together,
> and a little child shall lead them. . . .
> They shall not hurt or destroy
> in all my holy mountain.
>   (Isa. 11:6, 9a)

The prophets were not alone in holding up this vision. Israel's wisdom literature also anticipates the coming of this nonviolent

society. Psalm 85:10 speaks of it poetically as the age in which
"justice and peace will embrace."

Although the psalmist and the prophets are speaking of a
messianic age in the distant future, they believed that this was a
historical future. Christians should remember that fundamental to
our religion is the claim that this future age has begun. We proclaim Jesus as Messiah and his appearance on earth as the beginning of the messianic age. If our proclamation is to have any
credibility, it must be accompanied by eschatological signs. The
primary sign of the eschaton is peace (*shalom*). At the very least, our
lives as individuals and as a community should incarnate to some
degree the *shalom* portrayed in the messianic visions of the prophets
and should bear witness to our passionate engagement in the effort
to realize a measure of this *shalom* on earth. If the lives of the
people of God, imperfect and sinful as they inevitably will be, bear
no relationship to this *shalom*, then the Jewish argument that the
absence of messianic signs invalidates the Christian claim that Jesus
is the Messiah takes on considerable credibility.

An objection might be raised to using the Old Testament's
understanding of God's love as a basis for world peace because of
the particularist and tribalistic way in which this love is interpreted. Although tribalistic interpretations of God's love probably
represent the dominant view in the Old Testament, there are also
passages that show Israel's understanding of God's love developing
in a universalistic direction. Isaiah's poem envisioning the coming
nonviolent age is an example:

> It shall come to pass in the latter days
> that the mountain of the house of the Lord
> shall be established as the highest of the mountains,
> and shall be raised above the hills;
> and all the nations shall flow to it,
> and many peoples shall come and say:
> "Come, let us go up to the mountain of the Lord,
> to the house of the God of Jacob;
> that he may teach us his ways
> and that we may walk in his paths."
> For out of Zion shall go forth the law,
> and the word of the Lord from Jerusalem.
> He shall judge between the nations,

and shall decide for many peoples;
and they shall beat their swords into plowshares,
and their spears into pruning hooks;
nation shall not lift up sword against nation,
neither shall they learn war any more.

(Isa. 2:2-4)

Although one might accuse the poet here of religious imperialism, there is little ground for an accusation of political imperialism. The poet portrays a time when all nations will worship Yahweh in Jerusalem, but no force, conquest or subjugation is involved. The people themselves say, "Come, let us go up to the mountain of the Lord." The Lord does not show partiality to Israel but judges between many nations and decides for many peoples. In other words, the poem envisions a time when all peoples willingly and freely acknowledge the reign of the philanthropic Yahweh, though not necessarily the rule of Israel. When this time comes, "Nation shall not lift up sword against nation, neither shall they learn war any more." From a Christian perspective, this vision has begun to be fulfilled in Jesus and its incipient universalism has been brought to fruition in Jesus' vision of the kingdom and in the universal mission of the church.

The Suffering God as the Reconciliation of
Justice and Love

The Old Testament reveals a struggle in the religious consciousness of Israel to resolve the tension between God the warrior for justice and God the loving Father and Mother who brings peace and reconciliation. Israel's continued experience of God as steadfast love, especially in times of Israel's own unfaithfulness, sheds light on this mystery and leads Israel to a radical conclusion: justice and love are reconciled and enabled to embrace through *suffering*—the suffering of God and, secondarily, of God's people. Israel comes to this conclusion, perhaps unprecedented in the history of religion, under the tutelage of prophets such as Jeremiah, Hosea and Second Isaiah.

Hosea portrays God suffering to reconcile justice and love:

How can I give you up, O Ephraim!
How can I hand you over, O Israel! . . .

> My heart recoils within me,
> my compassion grows warm and tender.
> I will not execute my fierce anger,
> I will not again destroy Ephraim;
> for I am God and not man,
> the Holy One in your midst,
> and I will not come to destroy.
>
> (Hos. 11:8-9)

Justice would require the annihilation of Israel, but God's loving heart recoils at the thought and so God suffers the pain of
Israel's sin.

The best Old Testament expression of suffering as the path
that leads to the reconciliation of justice and love is perhaps found
in the servant songs of Second Isaiah, of which Isa. 53:5-6 is the
most profound and familiar.

> But he was wounded for our transgressions,
> he was bruised for our iniquities;
> upon him was the chastisement that made us whole,
> and with his stripes we are healed.

Although this passage speaks of the suffering of God's servant and
God's people, this whole section of Isaiah clearly portrays God as in
solidarity with the suffering servant. God's redemptive purposes
are accomplished through this suffering.

This understanding of suffering as the means through which
God reconciles justice and love is connected to the growing universalism of Israel's vision of redemption. This connection is expressed
in Isaiah 49:6, where God holds up the suffering servant as savior
not only of Israel but of all nations.

> "It is too light a thing that you should be my servant
> to raise up the tribes of Jacob
> and to restore the preserved of Israel;
> I will give you as a light to the nations,
> that my salvation may reach to the end of the earth."
>
> (Isa. 49:6)

These passages from Isaiah foreshadow the Passion of Jesus
and Paul's theology of the cross, the ultimate biblical expressions of
the belief that suffering is the path God has chosen to overcome
the tension between justice and love. They thus lead directly into a

consideration of the place of Jesus in the Christian understanding
of God and God's purpose for the world. However, we must first
consider one other conclusion about God and God's relationship to
the world to which Israel was led through its historical journey.

THE BIBLICAL GOD OF CREATION

Reflecting on its experience, Israel concluded early in its history that Yahweh was not only the redeemer of Israel, Yahweh was
also the creator of the universe! This understanding of God as
creator is already present in the Yahwist (ca. 900 B.C.E.) and no
doubt was not originated by him but was found in the tradition on
which he relied.

This theology of creation is expressed quite strongly in wisdom
literature, in some prophetic oracles and in such New Testament
books as John, Colossians and Ephesians. Biblical scholarship,
however, has often minimized the importance of the theology of
creation for Israel's and the church's religious vision. This has led
to a neglect of the theology of creation in the Western church
especially. One result of this neglect has been a separation of
redemption and creation, resulting in dualisms of nature and grace,
matter and spirit, politics and religion. An almost exclusive emphasis on redemption to the neglect of creation has radically narrowed
our understanding of redemption. Redemption in much of Western
theology has been understood as redemption from, rather than of,
creation. Thus, a subtle form of Gnosticism has come to prevail. I
believe an authentic witness to the biblical faith requires a recov-
ery of this biblical theology of creation and a reaffirmation of
creation, redemption and transformation as the *one, ongoing, inseparable* work of God.[31] A renewed understanding of the unity of
God's threefold work is also essential for the sake of social ethics
and ecumenical dialogue within the Christian tradition and
between Christianity and other religions. In light of the growing
integration of the human species, and of the need for a more
comprehensive and universal religious vision, such dialogue is
increasingly important in our time.[32]

The biblical process of joining faith in God as creator to faith
in God as redeemer was not easy. The existing creation mythology

was profoundly polytheist and, more importantly, the picture of divinity portrayed in these myths was contradictory to the image of God that prevailed in Israel. The creator-gods of ancient Near Eastern myths often achieved their purposes only after prolonged battle with divine adversaries. Creation itself frequently was seen as an afterthought, as in the *Enuma Elish,* where it is Marduk's way of cleaning up the mess after his battle with Tiamat—the victorious god cuts up the body of his defeated adversary and makes the world out of the pieces. Such mythology was incompatible with Israel's belief in the unchallengeable sovereignty of God experienced in the exodus. Attributing creation to Yahweh, therefore, required radical revision of existing mythology to conform to Israel's experience and understanding of Yahweh. It also led to a radically revised understanding of creation itself. The Yahwist and the theologians of the priestly tradition undertook the task of providing Israel with a theology of creation that was compatible with its understanding of Yahweh as redeemer and liberator.

For biblical theology, creation is not an afterthought or accident by God; God chose to create the world. Creation is, therefore, a self-expression of God. As such, material creation is not, as in many religious traditions, a falling away from God's goodness but an expression and incarnation of it. Creation is a sacrament of God. The biblical accounts of creation, especially the priestly account in Genesis 1, emphasize the goodness of material creation. In Genesis, God paused after each creative act and saw "that it was good." On the last day of creation, viewing all that God had made, God saw that "it was very good" (RSV). On this day God also assigns a special place in creation to humanity, giving to Adam and Eve "dominion" over all created things.[33] The second creation story speaks of the dignity and goodness of creation by portraying in anthropomorphic language God's personal and intimate relationship to and involvement in it (Gen. 2:7-9, 15, 18). Humanity's stewardship responsibilities are emphasized in the commission God gives to Adam to till and keep the garden (Gen. 2:15).

The process of integrating creation theology and exodus-inspired redemption theology is never quite completed in either the Old Testament or the New Testament, but there are examples of attempts at integration. For example, the social order that the

Torah regulations are intended to preserve is understood in Psalms 19 and 82 and elsewhere as part of a larger cosmic order, the order of *shalom*. Disruptions of the social order through injustice, oppression or war threaten the whole cosmos with chaos,[34] a thought that takes on a new and literal meaning in the nuclear age.

Paul offers perhaps the most profound biblical insight into the relationship between God's creative and redemptive work in his eschatological reflections in Romans, Colossians and Ephesians. For Paul the ultimate means of redemption is clearly the transfiguring love of God released with eschatological power in the life, death and resurrection of Jesus. Jesus' suffering is also the suffering of God, since God is in Christ, reconciling the world to God. Through this suffering love of Jesus, the whole created order, the *ta panta* (all things) of Colossians, is redeemed and reconciled (Eph. 1:10). The whole creation, says Paul, retains the hope of being freed, like us, from its slavery to decadence, to enjoy the same freedom and glory as the children of God. "From the beginning till now the entire creation, as we know, has been groaning in one great act of giving birth; and not only creation, but all of us who possess the first fruits of the Spirit, we too groan inwardly as we wait for our *bodies* to be set free" (Rom. 8:21-24, Jerusalem Bible).

This eschatological vision understands redemption in Christ not as redemption *from* creation but redemption *of* creation, or, in the words of Krister Stendahl, as "the mending of creation." It is better, I think, to speak of the consummation or completion of creation, since the end is more than the beginning. Irenaeus points this out when he speaks of the incarnation as something that would have occurred even if Adam had not sinned.[35] A theology that includes a vision of the transfiguration of the whole created universe cannot accept the idea that economic injustice or nuclear holocaust do not really matter because such an idea assumes that matter and the body are essentially unredeemable and destined for destruction.

The Bible's theology of creation and its completion in the doctrine of the Incarnation lead to quite the opposite assumption. The meaning of this theology for the future of creation will be illumined in the following chapters.

5

JESUS, GOD AND
THE KINGDOM

I have spoken at length about Israel's religious experience and its resulting understanding of God because this is the context within which the life, death and resurrection of Jesus and the New Testament community's experience of God in Jesus must be understood. Although Jesus leads his followers into new experiences and awarenesses of God that are beyond the parameters of Israel's religious experience, he does so by fulfilling and radicalizing the most radical aspects of that experience.

In this chapter I reflect on the life and ministry of the "historical Jesus," that is, Jesus before his arrest and execution. Christian theology often appears to attach little significance to the life of Jesus, and the creeds of the church ignore it altogether, skipping from his birth to his death. This is a great misfortune. One of the most important tasks of contemporary theology is to fill in this gap between Jesus' birth and death and to articulate the saving significance of the life of Jesus. Failure to perceive the importance of the historical Jesus for a proper understanding of Christian faith and life greatly increases the risk that Christianity will be understood as a "religion" in the narrow sense[1] and be used by the rulers of society to legitimize their position and, in the words of Karl Marx, as an "opium of the people."[2] Whenever the concrete and irreducible historical reality of Jesus of Nazareth is seriously studied and affirmed as the foundation of the Christian faith, the use of Christianity to legitimize an unjust status quo is impossible.[3] It is with these considerations in mind that this chapter is devoted to a discussion of the historical Jesus and his movement.[4]

THE QUESTS FOR THE
HISTORICAL JESUS

For more than a millennium and a half questions about the pre-ecclesial Jesus and his movement played no role in faith, church or theology. The historical accuracy of the picture of Jesus painted by the dogma, liturgy, art and piety of the church was naïvely and uncritically accepted. This was bound to be the case in a precritical age, when the dividing line between history and myth or Jesus and church was only vaguely perceived.

With the advent of the critical methodologies of the Renaissance and their application to the study of history, the question of the distinction between the historical Jesus and the Jesus of the church became a possibility. When Herman Samuel Reimarus, a professor of Oriental languages, applied these methodologies to a study of the Gospels in the eighteenth century, the quest for the historical Jesus began.[5] The first phase of this quest was concluded when Albert Schweitzer published his epochal book, *The Quest of the Historical Jesus.*[6] The reaction to Schweitzer's book was dramatic. Most scholars quickly abandoned the quest, claiming that Schweitzer had discredited it by showing that scholars had interpreted Jesus in terms of the ideals and values of modern Western society in general and their own philosophical or theological preferences in particular. However, this explains only part of the reaction to Schweitzer's book. In fact, what frightened many scholars was the picture that Schweitzer painted of the historical Jesus. Although subsequent research indicates that much of that picture is highly problematic, nevertheless Schweitzer's picture of Jesus is far more compatible with Gospel texts than those drawn by many of his predecessors. It is also less compatible with the ideas, values and goals of modern Western society. Schweitzer presents Jesus as an apocalyptic figure who exposed the hypocrisy and denounced the pride of his own society and who announced its end and the coming of a new order, the kingdom of God. Moreover, Schweitzer asserts that Jesus did not understand the kingdom in the exclusively spiritual and interior way that would have made it acceptable to the enlightened and liberal Western thinkers of Schweitzer's time.

The quest for the historical Jesus was not seriously resumed until 1954. In that year, Ernst Käsemann initiated the second stage of this quest, which is known as the new quest for the historical Jesus.[7] The new quest differs from the original one in three important ways. First, it is aware of the impossibility of constructing a biography of Jesus as we normally understand biography, and it generally rejects what was a very important goal of the first quest, the reconstruction of Jesus' inner life, his self-consciousness or self-understanding. Second, it believes that nevertheless some things can be said with near-certainty about the historical Jesus and that these things give us glimpses of the pre-ecclesial Jesus.

Finally, the new quest believes that these glimpses of the pre-ecclesial Jesus are very important for a proper understanding of Christianity because Christianity is intended to be a continuation of what the historical Jesus began. Therefore, doctrines and ethics that present themselves as Christian must be compatible with what is most certain about the historical Jesus and not mere creations of the church. This does not mean that the church can only repeat what Jesus said or did or that any particular doctrine or ethic is wrong, since in the power of the Spirit the believing community continues to ponder the meaning of Jesus and to understand it more fully and deeply.[8] It does mean, however, that it must be possible to show that Christian doctrine and ethics do not contradict the life and teaching of the historical Jesus as we can reconstruct them.

The new questers cannot use much of the work of the early quest, but one discovery of that movement remains of great importance. At the center of Jesus' proclamation and work is the announcement that the kingdom of God is breaking out here and now on earth, that the messianic age is dawning. This means that the focus of Jesus' ministry is not himself but God and God's reign on earth. This insight, widely accepted in theology today, is the basis for the present movement from a christocentric theology to a theocentric christology.[9]

JESUS' KINGDOM VISION

New Testament scholar Norman Perrin wrote, "The central aspect of the teaching of Jesus was that concerning the Kingdom of God. Of this there can be no doubt and today no scholar does, in fact, doubt it. Jesus appeared as one who proclaimed the Kingdom. All else in his message and ministry serves a function in relation to that proclamation and derives from it."[10] John Dominic Crossan, a Catholic New Testament scholar who has done groundbreaking work on the parables, expresses well this consensus about the historical Jesus that is developing among theologians today.[11] It has been easier to achieve this consensus than it has been to reach an agreement about Jesus' *understanding* of the kingdom. Does Jesus announce the arrival of the kingdom here and now—that is, as initiated by his ministry—or does he see the kingdom coming at some future time? Does Jesus see the kingdom as a supernatural reality established by God's intervention at the end of history, as an inner spiritual experience available now through conversion and faith, or as a social and political entity like the one that the prophets predicted and that Martin Luther King, Jr., envisioned and referred to as the "Beloved Community"? Does Jesus see the kingdom coming gradually within human history or appearing suddenly and bringing the end of history?

Recent studies focusing especially on Jesus' language suggest that God's kingdom transcends these dichotomies. Bernard Brandon Scott, for example, in *Jesus, Symbol-Maker for the Kingdom,* implies that these different ideas about the kingdom reflect the limitations of discursive language, which is logical, either/or language. Jesus' parables, reflecting his vision of the kingdom, transcend his language. They do not define the kingdom or describe it, but offer glimpses of it. Sometimes they present the kingdom in one way, and sometimes in another: sometimes they offer a this-worldly view, other times an other-worldly one. Sometimes continuity is emphasized, other times discontinuity; sometimes suddenness, sometimes gradualness; sometimes the inner, other times the outer dimension.[12]

Therefore, while it is necessary and fruitful to speak in logical terms about the kingdom of God, ultimately the vision of God's reign cannot be expressed or comprehended in discursive language. Rather, for Jesus, God's reign is both a realization of all our authentically human and Christian hopes and dreams—esthetic, ethical, economic, political and spiritual—and also much more than we have ever dreamed of or hoped for. That is why Jesus speaks of the kingdom symbolically and poetically. And although for Jesus the consummation of the kingdom is always ahead of us as a promise, he often emphasizes its present nearness. God's reign is breaking forth here and now, overthrowing oppressive religious and political oligarchies and social orders and establishing a new community of mutuality and solidarity in the midst of the old. It is precisely this emphasis on God's reign as a present reality that led to Jesus' conflict with the Roman and Jewish establishments.[13]

The good news that Jesus proclaimed and lived was that the reign of God on earth was beginning. What is the nature of this reign or kingdom of God that Jesus announced? Jesus did not prepare and present to the world a description of the kingdom of God or a political program designed to transform society into the kingdom. Perrin is right in saying that everything Jesus said and did is related to the kingdom. Most of Jesus' sayings and acts, however, are metaphorical and reflect his vision and understanding of the kingdom only indirectly. Nevertheless, studies of Jesus' teaching and acts have illumined many of the characteristics of the kingdom as Jesus envisioned it.

The Parables: Glimpses of the Kingdom

Some studies have focused on the parables of Jesus in the belief that these parables are unique in the history of religious literature and therefore reflect the uniqueness of Jesus' own religious vision. They are windows through which the hearer can glimpse the kingdom as Jesus sees it. Scott writes, "Parables, expressing the incomprehensible in terms of the comprehensible, are developed out of Jesus' fundamental vision or experience of reality."[14] What Scott and others are saying is that there are particularly intimate relationships between the person of Jesus and his parables and between his parables and his vision of the kingdom. The parables employ poetic language, which contributes to this intimacy because poetic language is by nature personal and closely connected to the experience of the one who uses it—especially if it evokes a highly original vision, as is the case in Jesus' parables.

The poetic nature of the parables led Perrin to conclude that for Jesus the kingdom was not an idea but a *symbol*, [15] a conclusion enthusiastically endorsed by Scott. A symbol, according to Perrin and Scott, is a metaphor with its ultimate referent suppressed. If we follow this line of reasoning, then the parables are Jesus' indirect way of speaking about the kingdom and the kingdom itself is the central symbol through which Jesus seeks to reveal the ultimate Reality which is so deep as to be inexpressible. Scott diagrams the relationship in this way:[16]

FIGURE 1

In this diagram, Jesus' experience of the ultimate referent (God, Abba) is expressed by the symbol "kingdom of God." The parables, in turn, are Jesus' way of shedding light on and clarifying the meaning of this symbol.

Given the special place of the parables as revelations of Jesus' way of seeing the kingdom of God, a good way to begin talking about Jesus' vision of the kingdom is to reflect on the parables. This is exactly what Crossan, Scott, Perrin and others do. Their work yields an awareness of the profoundly radical nature of Jesus' vision of the kingdom.

An excellent example of the fruit of this approach is found in Crossan's interpretation of the parable of the Good Samaritan. Crossan writes,

It is important that it is precisely a Samaritan who performs the good deed. If Jesus wanted to teach love of neighbor in distress, it would have sufficed to use the standard folkloric threesome and talk of one person, a second person and a third person. If he wanted to do this and add a jibe against the clerical circles of Jerusalem, it would have been quite enough to have mentioned priest, Levite, and let the third person be a Jewish lay person. Most importantly, if he wanted to inculcate love of enemies, it would have been radical enough to have a Jewish person stop and assist a wounded Samaritan. But, when the story is read as one told by the Jewish Jesus to a Jewish audience and presumably in a Jerusalem setting, this original historical context demands that the Samaritan be intended and heard as the socio-religious outcast which he was. . . . Hence the internal structure of the story and the historical setting of Jesus' time agree that the literal point of the story challenges the hearer to put together two impossible and contradictory words for the same person: "Samaritan" and "Neighbor." The whole thrust of the story demands that one say what cannot be said, what is a contradiction in terms: good plus Samaritan. On the lips of Jesus the story demands that the hearer respond by saying the contradictory, the impossible, the unspeakable. The point is not that one should help the neighbor in need. In such an intention the naming of the helper as a Samaritan before a Jewish audience would be un-necessary, distracting and, in the final analysis, inimical and counterproductive. For such a purpose it would have been far better to have made the wounded man a Samaritan and the helper a Jewish man outside clerical circles. But when good (cleric) and bad (Samaritan) become respectively bad and good, a world is being challenged and we are faced with polar reversal.[17]

Having discovered over and over again this kind of radical vision in the parables, Crossan concludes that Jesus' parables challenge the deep structures of the human psyche and human experience. In so doing, I believe they also challenge the social systems of humanity, which are external and institutional projections of these deep structures.

In *Jesus, Symbol-Maker for the Kingdom*, Scott continually reminds his readers that because the parables are poetic and vision-ary language, which participates in the reality it communicates, their meaning cannot be abstracted. Form and content are inseparable; when it comes to Jesus' parables, the medium truly is the message.[18] Nevertheless, on the basis of a study of eight representative parables, Scott attempts to extrapolate what he calls a grammar of parables. This grammar, which is the basic linguistic structure of Jesus' parables, points to Jesus' personal vision of reality.

Figure 2, which combines and adapts several of Scott's diagrams,[19] contrasts Jesus' vision of the kingdom as expressed in the imagery of four of his parables with the official vision of the kingdom as expressed in the imagery of the Jewish religious establishment. For the established religion, the prevailing images of the kingdom were the Great Tree (cedar of Lebanon) and unleavened bread (Exod. 12:17-20).[20] For Jesus, the symbols were a mustard plant (Ezek. 17:23; Matt. 13:31-32; Mark 4:30-32; Luke 13:18-19) and leavened bread (Matt. 13:33; Luke 13:20-21). These symbols are not merely different, they are contradictory. They lead in opposite directions. Those who picture the kingdom in terms of the great cedar of Lebanon or as unleavened bread, a symbol for righteousness, are led in the direction of self-righteous religion and prideful legalism. Those who picture the kingdom in terms of the mustard seed and leavened bread are led in the direction of humility, solidarity, servanthood and grace. This radical contrast between Jesus' images of the kingdom and the images of the established religion, found in parable after parable, points to an equally radical contrast in the kingdom visions that lie behind these images. It also explains why Jesus and his teachings were so controversial and

A_1 Kingdom of God (Religious Establishment)	B_1 Kingdom of God (Jesus)
A_2 Great Tree	B_2 Mustard Plant
A_3 Unleavened Bread	B_3 Leavened Bread
A_4 Samaritan as Opponent	B_4 Samaritan as Helper

FIGURE 2

why so many of his contemporaries found him shocking or enig-
matic. In this context, Jesus' oft-repeated statement, "He who has
ears to hear, let him hear" (Mark 4:9, 29; 7:16; Luke 8:8; 14:23,
e.g.), begins to make more sense.

Scott attempts to summarize what he has learned about the
grammar of Jesus' parables in another chart (Figure 3). As this
chart illustrates, the parables of Jesus reveal the reign of God as
grace open to all. The vision of the kingdom presented in Jesus'
parables is a vision of reality as an open, united and interconnected
whole. The parables invite the hearer to enter this reality and
become a part of it.

All these images of Jesus' parables are contrary to the established religion's vision of the kingdom as consisting of the
"accepted," those who embrace the correct theology and morality.
This establishment view of the kingdom presents a vision of reality
as divided—the kingdom is bestowed on the religiously orthodox
and the morally righteous (the accepted), while heretics and sin-

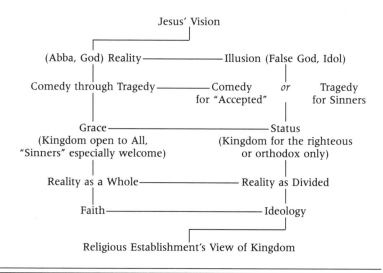

FIGURE 3

ners are rejected and condemned. In the establishment view, the kingdom is comedy for the accepted and tragedy for the rejected. For Jesus, the kingdom is comedy (resolution, resurrection, reconciliation) achieved through tragedy (suffering, dying) for all (potentially).[21]

These studies of the parables have done much to recover something of the radical vision of the pre-ecclesial Jesus. The modern quest for the historical Jesus does not limit itself, however, to a study of the parables. Although the parables may be the most strikingly unique expressions of Jesus' teaching, the other words and teachings of Jesus also reveal something of his uniqueness. In addition, Jesus' actions as reported in the Synoptics contribute important insights to our understanding of the historical Jesus. As Crossan says,

> There is more to Jesus' life than the parables. . . . He was not crucified for parables but for ways of acting which resulted from the experience of God presented in the parables. In this regard, the parables are cause and not effect of Jesus' other words and deeds. They are not what Joachim Jeremias called "weapons of warfare." They are the cause of the war and the manifesto of its inception.[22]

If Crossan is correct, then the unique and radical vision of God and God's reign found in the parables should also be expressed in Jesus' other sayings and in his actions.

The Kingdom in Jesus' Life and Words

I began the discussion of Jesus' parables by pointing out the broad consensus among New Testament scholars that the center of Jesus' message is the proclamation that the kingdom of God has come. Juan Luis Segundo, E. P. Sanders and others have shown that the kingdom is also the center of Jesus' nonparabolic teachings and of his actions. Indeed, a sense of the immediacy of the kingdom permeates all Jesus' sayings and actions. This sense is the primary basis of Sanders's conclusion that Jesus was not a mere religious reformer but an eschatological prophet who predicted and, in his attack on the temple, symbolically portrayed the coming destruction of the present religious, social and political order and the establishment of God's reign on earth.[23] According to Sanders, it was this eschatological zeal and the threat it posed to the order presided over by the Romans and chief priests that led to Jesus' execution.

Jesus' sayings and actions offer an explicit vision of what life and relationships in the kingdom are like and how they differ from life and relationships in the world as it is presently structured. Because they do this, Jesus' sayings and above all his actions frighten and threaten those who preside over the structures of this world and administer life in it.

THE SOCIAL IMPLICATIONS OF
JESUS' VISION

Segundo points out that Jesus' vision of the kingdom, although essentially a religious vision, has profound implications for society. For example, Jesus' vision of the kingdom is good news for the poor and all oppressed and marginalized groups. It is, however, usually perceived as bad news by those who enjoy power, riches and privilege in the present order. If we take the words of Jesus seriously and refrain from spiritualizing them, it is not hard to understand why this is the case.

According to Mark, Jesus begins his public ministry with the proclamation, "The time has come; the kingdom of God is upon you; repent and believe the gospel" (Mark 1:15, New English Bible). Luke portrays Jesus as beginning his public ministry by preaching a sermon based on Isaiah 61 in which, according to some commentators, he proclaims a jubilee year.[24] A jubilee year requires the cancellation of all debts, the freeing of all slaves, and the return of all property to its original owners. In Matthew, Jesus' public ministry begins with the Sermon on the Mount. This great discourse provides us with concrete notions of how we are to change our outlook and behavior in light of the kingdom's approach. The Beatitudes—particularly Luke's version, which most scholars think is more original—reveal that more than a radical change in religious outlook and behavior is required; political, economic, psychological and social perceptions and behaviors must also change radically. And how could it be otherwise? If our religious vision is, as it ought to be, the milieu from which we perceive and relate to all reality, then a radical change in that vision will alter our way of seeing and relating to the whole world in an equally radical way. The Beatitudes reflect this radically new way of seeing and relating to the world.

> Blessed are you poor, for yours is the kingdom of God.
> Blessed are you that hunger now, for you shall be satisfied.
> Blessed are you that weep now, for you shall laugh.
> Blessed are you when men hate you and when they exclude
>   you and revile you . . .
> for so their fathers did to the prophets.
>
> (Luke 6:20-23)

What Jesus is saying here is that the kingdom that is now arriving will effect a great social reversal. Those who are now poor will be blessed because the kingdom will belong to them. Likewise, the situation of those who weep and those who are persecuted will be reversed because the kingdom will belong to them. In order to leave no doubt about what he is saying, Jesus adds some words of woe:

> But woe to you that are rich, for you have received your
>   consolation.
> Woe to you that are full now, for you shall hunger.
> Woe to you that laugh now, for you shall mourn and weep.
> Woe to you when all men speak well of you, for so their
>   fathers did to false prophets.
>
> (Luke 6:24-26)

Jesus and the Poor

How should those who truly believe these words of Jesus respond? According to Jesus, saying "Lord, Lord" is not enough. He suggests that they renounce all efforts to accumulate worldly goods and embrace a life style based on the values of simplicity and solidarity. In other words, belief in these words of Jesus is expressed economically in solidarity with the poor. The gift of freedom received through believing Jesus' good word that the kingdom has come enables believers to live these Beatitudes by letting go of their possessions for the sake of that kingdom.

From this belief in Jesus' good word that the kingdom of God has come, a number of Jesus' other words and actions are explained. If the kingdom has come, for example, then Jesus' promise that those who leave their houses, families, possessions and reputations and become wandering prophets of the kingdom (Mark 10:29-30) will be rewarded in this world and in the world to come makes sense.[25] A positive response to this call is simply an expression of faith in the truth of Jesus' proclamation and therefore in the truthfulness and authenticity of the Proclaimer. True faith is risking everything. It is letting go of property and, in certain circumstances, of life itself, trusting only in the truthfulness of Jesus' proclamation and of the Proclaimer himself. The story of the rich young ruler (Mark 10:17-22) illustrates how difficult—indeed, impossible—it is to respond to this call without faith in Jesus' proclamation.

As Gerd Theissen points out, although such radicality was not required of all members of the Jesus movement, they were expected to understand and respect the life style of Jesus' wandering disciples and to prepare themselves spiritually and psychologically for such a life of renunciation—even, in fact, to expect it. They were to turn away from the accumulation of wealth and to share their possessions with the poor, who were to be accorded special honor in their communities.[26] Anyone who fell away from this life style and came under the power of greed, becoming indifferent toward the suffering of the poor, betrayed lack of faith in Jesus and in his proclamation and therefore placed himself or herself in the gravest spiritual danger. Many of Jesus' sayings warn of this danger. Two of the most powerful of these warnings are the parable of Lazarus and the Rich Man (Luke 16:19-31) and the words of Jesus in Mark 10:23-24 warning of the danger of riches.

Jesus himself adopts this way of life, becoming a wanderer without home, possessions or family (Matt. 8:20) and with no job, only a vocation to proclaim the coming of a new order. The crowds the Synoptics picture surrounding him and hanging on his every word probably included a disproportionate number of the poor.[27] Jesus' miracles for the most part were performed for the benefit of the poor.[28] According to the Gospels, the poor and other socially marginalized and outcast groups were especially attracted to Jesus and his vision of the kingdom. That is why, as Theissen says, "We keep meeting outsiders in the tradition: the sick and crippled, prostitutes and good-for-nothings, tax collectors and prodigal sons."[29]

Jesus' own life and his association with the dispossessed is consistent with those sayings that express the economic implications of his radical kingdom vision. A life of this sort makes sense only from the perspective of faith that the kingdom has come, because this is kingdom living.

Jesus and Women

Jesus profoundly challenged the mores and taboos of his society regarding the place of women and the relationship between men and women. Leonard Swidler points out that Jesus often used women as central figures in his stories and sayings, always in a positive way. He also shows that Jesus frequently juxtaposed two similar images or stories, one featuring a woman and the other a man (e.g., Matt. 13:31-33; Luke 15:3-32).[30] Jesus' frequent use of women as central figures in his teaching points to the fact that in the kingdom that is now at hand patriarchal social structures will be overcome and true mutuality will prevail between the sexes.

Some of Jesus' stories and sayings emphasize a particular dimension of male/female mutuality—namely, a woman's right to a spiritual and intellectual life of her own. Although Jesus affirmed marriage and family life, he insisted that personal, spiritual bonds were more important than familial bonds.[31] More specifically, he rejected explicitly the ideas that women are to be confined to the role of wife and mother and that they should seek to find recognition through their husbands and male offspring. In response to a woman who, moved by his teaching, cried, "Blessed is the womb that bore you and the breasts that you sucked," Jesus said, "Blessed rather are those who hear the word of God and keep it!" (Luke 11:27-28). Surely, blessedness is no more the result of biological function for women than for men. For both men and women, blessedness comes from hearing the word of God and doing it—in other words, through one's relationship with ultimate and transcendent reality.[32] The story of Mary and Martha (Luke 10:38-42) is also a strong defense of a woman's right to an intellectual and spiritual life. Luke pictures Mary sitting at Jesus' feet—the posture of a disciple. When Martha criticizes her sister for not being in the kitchen, Jesus defends her right to be a disciple and tells Martha that her sister has made the right choice.

Women and the actions of women appear also as images of the kingdom and of God. For example, the action of the woman who mixed the leaven in the flour (Luke 13:20-21) points to the coming of the kingdom. The woman who upon finding her lost coin invites her friends to celebrate with her is an image of the joy God feels when a broken relationship with one of God's children is healed (Luke 15:8-10). Jesus even applies female imagery to himself and his work in Luke 13:34, where he compares himself to a mother hen who desires to gather her chicks under her. In John 7:37-39, he again applies female imagery to himself when he invites those who are thirsty to come and drink from him. As Swidler points out, "The image of drinking from a human being can only be that of a mother."[33]

As with his sayings relating to kingdom economics, Jesus' sayings concerning the role of women and the nature of male/female relationships in the kingdom are lived out and interpreted in his actions. Luke 13:10-17 tells of Jesus' healing of a crippled woman in the synagogue on the Sabbath. Although Jesus' Sabbath healings always provoked attacks by his opponents, the attack in this case seems particularly vicious, perhaps because the religious indignation on the part of the ruler of the synagogue was reinforced by sexism. Jesus' defense of his action is also particularly strong: "Hypocrites! Is there one of you who does not untie his ox or his donkey from the manger on the Sabbath and take it out for a watering? And this woman, a daughter of Abraham, whom Satan held bound for eighteen years—was it not right to untie her bonds on the Sabbath?" (Luke 13:15-16, Jerusalem Bible). Swidler points out that while the title "son of Abraham" is used throughout Jewish literature to refer to a male member of the chosen people, the phrase "daughter of Abraham" as a title of honor for a woman rarely occurs.[34] Jesus' use of this term reflects his vision of the kingdom as a reality in which women participate fully and in true mutuality with men.

Another of Jesus' miracles illustrates how he lived out his vision of the equality of women in the kingdom. All the Synoptics report Jesus' healing of a woman with a constant flow of blood (Matt. 9:20-22; Mark 5:25-34; Luke 8:43-48). This woman touched Jesus as he was on his way to heal the daughter of Jairus and was herself healed. Because of the blood that flowed from her, she would have been considered unclean and those touched by her would have had to undergo ritual purification. Jesus, however, not only does not rebuke the woman for touching him, but calls attention to her and her cure and praises her. There is no indication that Jesus underwent a ritual purification before proceeding to the house of Jairus. Swidler suggests that this story reveals a rejection by Jesus of the idea that a woman with a flow of blood, menstrual or otherwise, is ritually unclean.[35] Whether or not this is true, Jesus' action is fully consistent with his kingdom vision and affirms the full humanity of women.

I conclude by pointing out one more fact, the most radical of all about Jesus' relationship with women: Jesus had female disciples! The story of Mary and Martha (Luke 10:38-42), to which I already referred, portrays Mary as a disciple. All the Synoptic Gospels mention women members of the band of disciples that traveled with Jesus through Galilee and from Galilee to Jerusalem. Luke, for example, writes, "With him went the Twelve as well as certain women who had been cured of evil spirits and ailments: Mary, surnamed the Magdalene, . . . Joanna, the wife of Herod's steward, Chuza, Susanna, and several others" (Luke 8:1-3, Jerusalem Bible).

In Mark and Matthew, only the women disciples remain with Jesus through the crucifixion. In the Synoptics it is only the women who go with Joseph of Arimathea to bury Jesus. And the Gospels are unanimous in asserting that women were the first to know of the resurrection and to see the risen Jesus. In the Gospel stories of the empty tomb and the appearance of the risen Jesus, the women are sent by angels or by Jesus himself to proclaim the resurrection to the disciples. The tradition has sometimes assigned these women disciples the title "apostles to the apostles." Mary Magdalene in particular, whose name appears in all of these texts and who always heads the list, has been referred to by this title.[36]

According to Swidler and others, in choosing women as the first witnesses to his resurrection and in sending them as apostles to the apostles, Jesus rejects first-century Palestinian Judaism's strictures against women serving as witnesses.[37] Indeed, Jesus commissions women to be the chief witnesses to the very event upon which the kingdom is founded—his resurrection from the dead. In so doing, Jesus challenges the hierarchical, patriarchal world order, not just in word but in deed, and replaces it with the order of the kingdom, which is based on mutuality between men and women and is open to full participation by women.

Jesus and Enemies

We have already seen how, in the parable of the Good Samaritan, Jesus radically challenged his society's vision of reality as divided into like and unlike, friend and enemy. Many of Jesus' nonparabolic sayings and actions communicate this same vision and make explicit the ethical implications of this vision for relationships with our enemies.[38] For Jesus, such a vision rules out a double standard of ethical behavior, one to regulate relations with enemies, another to guide relations with friends. Those who follow Jesus are to be guided in their dealing with all people, friends as well as enemies, by a single ethical standard—love.

Jesus' most direct application of the kingdom vision to the question of ethical relations with enemies is in the Sermon on the Mount (Matt. 5:38-48; Luke 6:27-37). Jesus cites the Torah: "If any harm follows, you shall give life for life, eye for eye, tooth for tooth, hand for hand, foot for foot, burn for burn, wound for wound, stripe for stripe" (Exod. 21:23-25). Then he offers his own teaching: "You have heard that it was said, 'An eye for an eye and a tooth for a tooth.' But I say to you, Do not resist one who is evil. But if one strikes you on the right cheek, turn to him the other also" (Matt. 5:38-39). This is one of the few instances in which the New Testament records a teaching of Jesus contradicting the Torah.

As William Klassen points out, even the most skeptical scholars, including Rudolf Bultmann, have admitted that the comment to "love your enemies"[39] goes back to Jesus himself. Klassen also points out that in spite of the efforts of the church and theologians to prove that Jesus meant personal enemies, not political or national enemies, scholars today generally agree that "neither the term love nor the term enemy can be restricted *in any way* if we want to do justice to what Jesus said."[40] Eduard Schweitzer in his commentary on Matthew also concludes regarding the application of this text that "there is not the slightest hint of any realm where the disciple is not bound by the words of Jesus."[41] As numerous church historians have pointed out, the pre-Constantinian church understood this far better than the established church after Constantine. According to Klassen, in the second century this command was the most quoted of all the sayings of Jesus.[42] Indeed, there is considerable evidence to suggest that in the early Christian community, love of enemies was the primary ethical mark distinguishing Christians from others. In those times "enemies" had a very concrete meaning for the Christian. Enemies were above all those who persecuted the Christian community and tried to exterminate the Christian faith. These were the people the early Christian communities felt called to love and to pray for in their public assemblies.

Once again, Jesus' words are incarnated in his actions. According to the Gospels, Jesus consistently rejected violence as a means to bring in the kingdom of God. Rather, he announced to his disciples that his would be the way of suffering love, the way of the cross. When Peter objected to this, Jesus rebuked him, saying, "Get behind me, Satan! Because the way you think is not God's way, but men's" (Mark 8:33b, Jerusalem Bible). On the night of Jesus' arrest, when Peter tried to defend him with a sword, Jesus again rebuked him, saying, "Put your sword back into its place; for all who take the sword will perish by the sword" (Matt. 26:52; par. Mark 14:47; Luke 23:49-51; John 18:10-11). The most dramatic example of Jesus' practice of loving his enemies is his prayer from the cross: "Father, forgive them, for they know not what they do" (Luke 23:34).

Jesus acknowledges and even emphasizes that he and those who follow him will have enemies who hate them and seek to do them harm. Indeed, many of Jesus' teachings, as well as the example of his own life, serve to warn Christians that the more faithfully they live by the kingdom vision the more enemies they will have. Moreover, Jesus emphasizes that love of enemy is perfectly consistent with opposition to the enemy. In fact, he often seems to imply that love *requires* such opposition and that opposition heightens the enmity (Matt. 10:16-22). Jesus' words and actions make it clear that cooperation with or resignation to what one believes is evil was not Jesus' way or the way to which he called his disciples. On the contrary, Jesus consistently denounced and confronted evil, as his bold attacks on the legalism of the Jewish religious establishment indicate.

Such actions as these, which occur frequently in the life of Jesus, make untenable Reinhold Niebuhr's interpretation of Jesus' words, "Do not resist evil" (Matt. 5:39). Niebuhr's insistence that Jesus' ethic "uncompromisingly enjoins non-resistance and not non-violent resistance"[43] and that Christians "will find nothing in the gospel that justifies non-violent resistance as an instrument of love perfectionism"[44] is contradicted by Jesus' behavior. If Jesus had really meant his words in this way, the Gospels would not be so filled with stories of controversy and Jesus would never have been crucified. Yet this interpretation of Jesus' teachings on non-resistance is one of the chief pillars on which Niebuhr rests his case that Jesus was not to the slightest degree "involved in the relativities of politics"[45] and that his teaching, therefore, has no immediate relevance for the practical problems with which society struggles.

A number of scholars have called both these assertions of Niebuhr into serious question. Segundo and, before him, G.H.C. MacGregor have raised significant objections to Niebuhr's reasoning on this matter.[46] More recently, Luise Schottroff has pointed out that "non-cooperation with evil . . . is not incompatible with Matthew 5:39, because Matthew 5:39 is not a fundamental rejection of *every* type of resistance."[47] This interpretation of Matt. 5:39 by Schottroff, MacGregor, Segundo and others is supported by many writings from the patristic period. For example, John Chrysostom writes, "What then, ought we not to resist evil? Indeed we ought but not by retaliation. Christ hath commanded us to give up ourselves to suffering wrongfully for thus we shall prevail over evil. For one fire is not quenched by another, but fire by water."[48]

Perhaps the modern disciple of Jesus who best comprehended and practiced this teaching regarding love of enemy was Mahatma Gandhi.[49] Gandhi understood that love of enemy did not mean "meek submission to the will of the evil doer but pitting one's whole soul against the will of the tyrant."[50] Gandhi also understood, however, that loving the enemy while simultaneously resisting evil required "self-suffering."[51] It is for this reason that E. Stanley Jones speaks of Gandhi's work as an effort to apply the power of the cross to politics.[52] Martin Luther King, Jr., Gandhi's best-known disciple, also was aware of the relationship between suffering and loving, nonviolent resistance of one's enemies. King often spoke of the comfort that came from the knowledge that he had cosmic company in his suffering.

Love of Enemy and Nationalism

The emphasis on love of enemy in Jesus' kingdom ethics presents a major problem for the nation-state political system. This system is built on a vision of reality as divided and is dependent for its continued existence on the tribalistic instincts of the human species. A vision like that of Jesus, especially when it is incarnated in a personal and political life style, undermines the very foundations of all tribalistic institutions, of which the nation-state is today the most prominent. Paul understood this very well and expressed it in those passages in which he speaks of Jesus' work as one of universal reconciliation (Eph. 2:1-22; Col. 1:15-20). The effect of Jesus' life, death and resurrection was to put an end to enmity, alienation and all forms of tribalism and to create *one new humanity*. What does it mean politically to the Roman Empire, the Soviet Union, the United States or any tribalistic institution that a community has emerged within it for which there can no longer be Greek, Jew, barbarian, Scythian, free or slave because Christ is all in all (Col. 3:11; cf. Rom. 10:11; Gal. 3:29; Eph. 2:11-22; Col. 1:5a-23)? The Roman emperors rightly perceived that such a community, if faithful to its vision, posed a lethal threat to the state. Both ecclesiastical and state records reveal that the Christian community was in fact sufficiently faithful to its vision to threaten the security of the state. Indeed, many—perhaps a majority—of pre-Constantinian Christians refused to participate in the wars of the state, giving as their reasons God's prohibition of all killing, the biblical understanding of every human being as image and likeness of God and the Christian belief that Jesus lived, died and arose to redeem all humanity.[53]

Even more threatening than Christians' disobedience of the state's command to kill was their rejection of the state's claim to divinity, since the state based its authority to command obedience of its citizens on this claim. Many Christians bore public and therefore political testimony to their rejection of the state's pretensions to divinity by refusing to burn incense to Caesar or to say *kaiser kurios* (Caesar is lord). This gesture was required of all Roman subjects and was similar in significance to our Pledge of Allegiance to the flag. This public defiance by Christians dissipated the mystique of divinity and omnipotence with which the state surrounded itself and upon which it relied to maintain its authority and to preserve the existing social structures and relationships.

The prophetic tradition of Israel began this process of demythologizing the state, but Jesus contributed significantly to it in word and deed. Jesus' response to certain Pharisees who warned him to flee Galilee because the king, Herod Antipas, sought to kill him indicates his attitude toward the state. "Go and tell that fox," said Jesus, "Behold, I cast out demons and perform cures today and tomorrow and the third day I finish my course" (Luke 13:31-32). In other words, the state did not set Jesus' agenda; he and his Father did.

In the context of a discussion on true greatness in Luke 22:24-26, Jesus points to the emperor Tiberius as an example of what greatness is *not*. Here the emperor personifies the vision and values upon which all the social structures and relationships of the Roman system are built: "The kings of the Gentiles exercise lordship over them; and those in authority over them are called benefactors. But not so with you; rather let the greatest among you become as the youngest and the leader as one who serves" (Luke 22:25-26). Although the emperor is not mentioned by name, inasmuch as "Benefactor" was one of his official titles and was printed on Roman coins, Jesus' hearers are likely to have known that he was referring to Tiberius and to Roman society.[54]

Perhaps the saying that most forcefully strips away the state's pretensions to divinity is Jesus' reply to the question about paying taxes (Matt. 22:17-21; Mark 12:14-17; Luke 20:22-25). Although Jesus offers an ambiguous answer, there is one point on which he is anything but ambiguous: Caesar is *not* God. Jesus' emphasis seems to be precisely on that point since to make a clear and decisive distinction, as Jesus does, between Caesar and God is to refute the state's explicit claim to divinity and to challenge the fundamental presupposition on which the Roman Empire and every other idolatrous nationalistic system is based. By clearly distinguishing Caesar from God and stripping Caesar of his divine pretension, Jesus rejects the vision of reality as divided, of which all idolatry is the religious expression. In its place, he offers a vision of reality as an undivided whole, flowing out of and returning to the one creating, redeeming and transfiguring God, to whom also Caesar belongs. Indeed, in this saying Jesus stands in the tradition of biblical faith's polemic against idolatry in every form, especially the idolatrous worship of the nation. From a negative point of view, biblical faith's greatest contribution to human evolution is its devastating attack on idolatry. Eric Fromm analyzes the dynamics of idolatry and concludes: "In idolatry one partial faculty of man is absolutized and made into an idol. Man then worships himself in alienated form."[55] In the case of the idolatry of the nation, power is the partial attribute of humanity that is absolutized and worshiped. In the Roman Empire, Caesar is the personification of this power and is the state in deified form. Jesus in the texts explodes this myth. By destroying idols, of which the nation is perhaps the most powerful, biblical faith frees human imagination and energy to serve the true God by participating joyfully in God's creating, redeeming and transfiguring activity. This activity is the function of the Love that is God, which humanity enters through faith.

Once again, Jesus incarnates his teaching in his actions. Richard Cassidy points to the lack of deference that characterized all Jesus' interactions with the Jewish and Roman rulers.[56] The clearest expression of this is found in the Gospels' description of Jesus' behavior at his arrest and trial. Throughout the story of the Passion, Jesus is sovereign over the situation. He takes charge of the arrest scene in the garden, instructing Peter to put away his sword. He takes the initiative away from the chief priests, temple police and elders by saying, "Have you come out as against a robber, with swords and clubs? When I was with you day after day in the temple, you did not lay hands on me. But this is your hour, and the power of darkness" (Luke 22:52-53; par. Mark 14:48-49; Matt. 26:55-56). Jesus' refusal to answer the questions of the Sanhedrin, his rebuke of the officer who slapped him and, by implication, of the high priest (John 18:22-23), and his silence before the Jewish high court and Pilate can be interpreted as signs of his refusal to cooperate with a process that was obviously unjust if not illegal. His answer to Pilate—"You would have no power over me unless it had been given you from above" (John 19:11)—places the power of the state in the proper perspective. It is a derived and therefore relative, not absolute, power.

In Jesus' actions as well as in his words, the nation is demoted to the status of a human institution intended to serve the cause of human well-being and accountable for its actions to God. When it betrays this God-given vocation, Christians are obliged to resist and disobey its commands. This demythologization and demotion of the state are closely related to the vision of undivided reality out of which Jesus' injunction to love the enemy flows. Nations, like all idols, divide. The Love that is God unites.

Jesus and Sinners

The kingdom vision of reality as undivided, communicated by Jesus' teaching and life, exposes the idolatry of all human institutions and ideologies. I have already pointed out that the implications of Jesus' vision for the economic life of individuals and societies expose the idolatry of money. Likewise, his kingdom vision exposed the idolatrous nature of male domination or patriarchy, and his teaching of universal love, including love of enemy, undermined idolatrous nationalism. Jesus' most direct and continuous attack, however, was directed against the fundamental idolatry of religion, which reveals the dynamics operative in all idolatry.

Religious idolatry can take many forms, but its most common expression is the absolutization of a particular belief system or morality. In idolatrous religion, absolutized doctrine or morality takes the place occupied by God in biblical faith. On the basis of an absolutized religious, theological, ecclesiastical, or moral system, humanity is divided into the just and sinners, the pure and the impure, the moral and the immoral, the true believers (orthodox) and the false believers (heterodox). Such a religion is, as Segundo has pointed out, an ideology and as such functions psychologically, sociologically and politically quite differently from biblical faith.[57] Segundo analyzes Jesus' attack on the religion of his society, which functioned as an idolatrous ideology, and argues that for Jesus religion was a secondary or relative value. What was of ultimate value for Jesus was human welfare.

One of the incidents upon which Segundo bases his case is Jesus' defense of his disciples' picking and eating grain on the Sabbath. Jesus responds, "The Sabbath was made for man, not man for the Sabbath" (Mark 2:27). According to Segundo, the point Jesus is making is clearly that the Sabbath (i.e., religion) is relative but human welfare is absolute.[58] Jesus justifies this reversal of religion and human welfare on the basis of his experience and understanding of God. Segundo states, "Everything of a 'religious' nature points to God. But the God of Jesus . . . points to human beings, their needs and their value."[59] Irenaeus expresses this same insight more poetically when he declares, "The glory of God is a human being fully alive." In light of this reversal of values, it comes as no surprise that the religious establishment viewed Jesus' teachings and actions as blasphemous and that they charged him with blasphemy at his trial before the Sanhedrin.[60] Nevertheless, Jesus continued to insist that it is not sacrifice but mercy that God desires.

Jesus translated his teaching about religion into action in the most dramatic way possible. He did not insist that the disciples observe the rules for ritual purification (Matt. 15:2); he performed and commanded others to perform acts on the Sabbath that at least some rabbis would have considered illegal (Luke 13:10-17; John 9:1-12); he rejected the idea of the relationship between sin and sickness and therefore the idea that the ill were unclean or sinners (John 9:1-4); and he associated with notorious sinners, especially prostitutes and tax collectors, who were considered thieves and traitors. What's more, he told stories and made statements in which the attitudes and behaviors of religious leaders compared negatively with those of notorious public sinners. One well-known example is the story of the Pharisee and the tax collector who went into the temple to pray (Luke 18:9-14). In a number of instances Jesus declared that prostitutes and tax collectors would enter the kingdom before the hypocrites who presided over society's established religious institutions (see, e.g., Matt. 21:31). At the banquet of Simon the Pharisee, no doubt to the horror of the righteous and religious guests, a woman from the streets entered, washed Jesus' feet with her tears, dried them with her hair and anointed them with oil. If Jesus were a righteous man, thought Simon, he would not allow such a woman to touch him. But Jesus defended her action and pointed to her great love as an example for Simon and his guests to follow (Luke 7:36-50). In John 8:3-11 Jesus comes to the aid of a woman who is to be stoned to death for an act of adultery. When asked for his advice, Jesus replies, "Let him who is without sin among you be the first to throw a stone at her" (John 8:7).

Jesus' vision of the kingdom dethrones all religious idolatries that divide people into sinners and righteous, right believers and heretics, religious and irreligious, believers and atheists. What matters in the kingdom is not religion, but *love*, fundamentally God's love but also that love as it is embodied in human persons and communities. As a corollary to this love, what matters in the kingdom is the welfare of human beings—indeed, I would say, of *all creation*, for God is the Creator of all and the Lover of all that God has made. God's concern for the welfare of all creation is ultimately rooted in the very innermost nature of God as Love. Segundo rightly discerns this to be the point of the debate between Jesus and his opponents in Matt. 12:22-32. The scribes from Jerusalem accuse Jesus of casting out demons by the power of the prince of demons. Jesus' response, according to Segundo, is, What difference does it make? If Satan is casting out demons then Satan is divided from himself and is about to fall. What matters is that a human being is restored to wholeness. Because God's cause and desire is always the healing and saving of human beings, God is the winner in such healings even if they are performed by Satan.[61] Matthew 25:31-46 makes a similar point: it is not confessing "Lord, Lord" or accepting all the orthodox dogma that matters in the kingdom but love, expressed in feeding the hungry, giving drink to the thirsty, clothing the naked, visiting those in prison and bringing good news to the poor.

Jesus' vision of the kingdom of God puts an end to religion as an ideology that separates humanity into the righteous and sinners. Rather, this vision invites all humanity and the entire cosmos into the one undivided reality of the God who is Love. Indeed, in

Jesus' vision it is precisely this love that overcomes all divisions, breaks down all barriers and reconciles all things under the benign reign of the one, creating, redeeming and transfiguring God (Col. 1:19-20). The call goes out from Jesus, "Repent and believe that this reign has come near," for through repentance and faith we enter into this kingdom and become a part of its coming.

6

THE POLITICAL SIGNIFICANCE OF JESUS' DEATH AND RESURRECTION

We have been weaving our way through the experience of the biblical faith community, focusing especially on those episodes that the community itself believed illumined the nature of God and God's purpose for the world in unusually clear and powerful ways and thereby shed light on its own mission. These episodes include the exodus, the Sinai/Torah event and the period of classical prophecy. We concluded this journey by talking about the historical Jesus because the Christian community's experience of Jesus is definitive for its understanding of God. In this discussion, the radicality of Jesus' experience and understanding of God emerged. This radicality was expressed in Jesus' parables, unique in the history of religious literature, and also in those instances in which Jesus spoke directly about God. As chapter 5 indicated, Jesus' language and imagery, as well as his life style and actions, reveal that his experience and understanding of God and God's reign on earth were very different from those of the Jewish and Roman religious and political establishment.

THE IMPLICATIONS
OF JESUS' EXPERIENCE OF GOD

Jesus' unique experience of God and vision of God's kingdom on earth have profound implications for living that are expressed in his teaching and life. Jesus' teaching in the Sermon on the Mount is the most obvious, but not the only, expression of the radical nature of these implications. In his own life, Jesus incarnated the implications of his experience and understanding of God for life in this world. In very concrete and dramatic ways, Jesus demonstrated the reality and the meaning of his proclamation that the kingdom of God has come to earth. He reached out to the excluded—women, the poor, the handicapped, the ritually unclean, lepers and other diseased persons, children and foreigners. In these actions, as well as in his words, Jesus unequivocally declared that such people are not only invited into the kingdom but will enjoy places of honor there. The kingdom of God *belongs* to such people, Jesus declared. Whores and thieves will enter the kingdom before the leaders of the religious and politico-economic establishment. Whoever would enter the kingdom must be a servant (Mark 9:35) and must become like a child (Luke 18:17). Jesus taught that the order of the kingdom reverses the prevailing metaphysical, ethical and social order because it challenges the understanding of God and God's will for the world upon which the legitimacy of that order is based.

Because the God of Jesus and the reign of this God on earth, as announced and actualized by Jesus, threatened the present world order and its rulers, a conflict broke out between them and Jesus, between their god and Jesus' God. The pages of the New Testament are full of stories about this conflict, which eventually led to Jesus' execution at the hands of the religious and political principalities and powers.

This conflict was fundamentally a metaphysical conflict between two opposed ways of experiencing, imaging and understanding God.[1] Since a community's religion, as its response to God, is based upon its experience and understanding of God, the conflict between Jesus and the established Jewish and Roman religions was a religious conflict. Jesus and these religions had different understandings of who God was and, therefore, of what authentic religion was. But the conflict between Jesus and the rulers of his society was not confined to metaphysical and religious issues. Of necessity it touched upon *every* dimension of personal and social life because, for Jesus, the community's experience of God was to be definitive not only for its religious life but also for its economic and political life and for the personal lives of each of its members. True religion was life in its totality based in faith and lived in covenant with the God whom Jesus experienced and revealed as Love. Jesus challenged the most fundamental metaphysical beliefs of his society. Without a doubt this challenge shook the foundations of that society's religious, political and economic structures, which were built on and legitimized by these beliefs. Karl Marx acknowledged the profound political importance of such a challenge to established religion when he wrote, "Criticism of religion is the premise of all [social] criticism."[2] The rulers of Jesus' society—the Jerusalem priesthood, the Herodians, some of the Pharisees and the Romans themselves—also understood this and acted politically to do away with Jesus, the blasphemer, rebel and disturber of the peace.[3] Therefore they arrested Jesus, brought him to trial, convicted and executed him.

Jürgen Moltmann points out that the fact that Jesus was condemned and executed by the political and religious authorities of his time as a threat to public order is of fundamental importance for our understanding of Jesus' ministry. Because Jesus died at the hands of these authorities, "His death must be understood in the context of the conflict between him and the world around him . . . thus his death is a 'consequence of his ministry.'"[4] From an historical and empirical point of view, Jesus' crucifixion was a political event. Jesus was executed as a political offender. All of the New Testament authors found enormous religious and metaphysical significance in Jesus' crucifixion, and rightly so. But if the metaphysical and religious interpretations of the cross are allowed to blot out its political dimension, we lose sight of a crucial aspect of the salvation accomplished through Jesus—the political aspect— and the prophetic and incarnational aspects of Christianity are also lost. An exclusively religious and metaphysical approach leads interpreters to conclude that Jesus' death "can scarcely be understood as an inherent and necessary consequence of his activity. Rather, it took place because his activity was misconstrued as political activity."[5] As Moltmann rightly points out, such a statement projects a nineteenth-century belief in the separation of religion and politics upon first-century Palestine.[6] In so tense a political situation, it would have been impossible for Jesus' public ministry to remain without political impact unless he had been concerned *exclusively* with inner dispositions. But as we have already seen, the tradition makes abundantly clear that Jesus was concerned also with external realities and relationships. It is not surprising, therefore, that for Pilate the case of Jesus of Nazareth was on the same level as that of Barabbas, the rebel captured in the insurrection.[7] To be sure, Pilate misunderstood Jesus. However,

> in the deeper sense of a challenge to the *Pax Romana* and its gods and laws . . . Pilate understood him aright. This is shown by the effect . . . the crucified man from Nazareth ultimately had upon the Roman Empire in the life of early Christianity. The worship of a crucified God contained a strictly political significance which cannot be sublimated into the religious sphere. The Christians' open rejection of emperor worship brought them martyrdom in a sense that was both religious and political.[8]

What Moltmann says about Jesus' challenge to the *Pax Romana* and its gods and laws is equally relevant for today's American or Soviet systems. The ultimate political significance of Jesus is that he relativizes the sovereignty claims of all human institutions, making them accountable to the authority of God. Furthermore, he points out some of the concrete implications that relativization has for political behavior. It is because many early Christians understood these political implications that they refused to burn incense to Caesar and to kill for him in his wars. Under these circumstances, Caesar could not help but perceive in the Christian community a fatal threat.

The political implications and effects of Jesus' work become still clearer when we realize that he shared many concerns with the Zealots, Jewish guerrillas fighting for freedom from Rome. Moltmann discusses six of these in his book *The Crucified God*.[9] Jesus himself was often seen as a Zealot and was probably crucified as one.[10] However, there is broad agreement among New Testament scholars that Jesus was not a Zealot but offered a new political and religious alternative that flowed from his very different experience and understanding of God and of God's ways in the world. Jesus believed and proclaimed that God establishes divine justice on earth not through law and judgment but through grace. God comes not to carry out revenge on the evil but to forgive and set them right. According to Moltmann, this reflects a revolution in the concept of God, from which all of Jesus' nonviolent teachings and actions are derived.[11] Just as God comes not to destroy but to forgive and set right God's enemies, so God's people are to forgive and love their enemies. Jon Sobrino clarifies this point. For Jesus, he says, power cannot be the ultimate mediation of God to the world because power tends to oppress. Over against this popular conception of God as a power, Jesus sets the notion of God as Love.[12] Yet for Jesus, the love of God is a *political* force because it always seeks to incarnate itself, that is, to be real and effective in a given concrete situation. The love of God as proclaimed and expressed by Jesus ceaselessly confronts and demolishes barriers that seek to confine and prevent its free flow not only in the realm of interior life, interpersonal relations and religion but also throughout society and the cosmos. Some of these barriers are attitudes, such as those toward personal, racial, cultural, class or national enemies or toward sinners. Jesus exhorts his followers to transcend these barriers by loving their enemies and sinners in concrete ways. Some barriers are behaviors, such as the behavior of the rich who store up treasures for themselves while their brothers and sisters starve, or the behavior of the powerless groups in society that passively accept and resign themselves to injustices inflicted upon them. Jesus exhorts those who hear him to change these behaviors. Some of these barriers are institutions and structures. Although Jesus' most explicit and developed critique of structural barriers to love was directed at the religious system, criticism of the economic and political systems is implicit and sometimes explicit in Jesus' ministry. Jesus seeks to free his followers from fear of and subservience to such structures and systems.

Jesus' understanding of God's love as a political force and his effective use of that force in society frightened the rulers and provoked them to take what they thought was definitive action against him. Paradoxically, however, Jesus' crucifixion became the ultimate expression of the power of Love (God) and the means through which that power overcame injustice and death. God as Love establishes justice on earth not only by fighting injustice but by suffering it; God overcomes death by dying in love. As Sobrino so aptly puts it, "In the cross God does not show up as one who wields power *over* the negative from the *outside;* rather, in the cross, the possibility of overcoming the negative is realized by submersion within the mechanisms and processes of the negative."[13] This understanding of the way God's redemptive energy works leads to a totally new concept of transcendence. The crucifixion of Jesus reveals that God is recognized and works in the world in ways that contradict our natural understanding of divinity based primarily on power, God is like Alexander the Great or Augustus Caesar. The crucifixion teaches us to image God as One who appears in the form of and works through suffering love. Justin Martyr expressed this awareness when, in response to the question, What does your God look like? he replied, "Like a crucified man."

The implications of this new image of transcendence for Christian spirituality, ethics and politics are profound. Those who see in the cross a revelation of God's nature and an illumination of God's ways of working in the world understand the central mystery of the Christian faith. The God of Jesus chooses to appear and be present in this world in suffering, especially in the suffering of the poor and oppressed and of those who struggle with them to realize the justice of God on earth (cf. Matt. 25:31-46; 1 Cor. 1:18-31). Those who desire to live in communion with this God will be drawn into solidarity with these suffering ones and into engagement in the struggle, because that is where the God of Jesus Christ, the God of the cross and the exodus, is to be found. However, as Sobrino rightly says, "The cross is not the last word on Jesus because God raised him from the dead."[14]

JESUS' RESURRECTION AND THE KINGDOM LIFE

How shall we understand the resurrection and its significance for Christian faith and life? The literature on this subject is enormous and opinions not only vary but are often contradictory.[15] In addition, there are so many different aspects to consider in any discussion of the resurrection.

One such aspect is the question of the historicity or nonhisto-ricity of this event. Wolfart Pannenberg's book *Jesus, God and Man* provides one of the clearest, most logical and consistent discussions of this question. While acknowledging the metaphorical nature of biblical language about the resurrection as well as the legendary elements of the appearance stories, Pannenberg concludes that the New Testament witness of the resurrection is fundamentally credi-ble historically. For Pannenberg, Jesus' resurrection must be desig-nated an historical event because the emergence of primitive Christianity cannot be understood apart from a hope for a resur-rection of the dead, a hope that for early Christians was firmly rooted in the belief in Jesus' resurrection.[16]

Pannenberg also illuminates the cognitive meaning of the res-urrection for our understanding of the future of humanity. Refer-ring to the theology of sacred history developed by Ignatius and Irenaeus, Pannenberg suggests that the new humanity that emerged in Jesus and was fully realized through his resurrection from the dead is, in fact, the actualization of the image of God in Genesis 1. Humanity as image of God is not something established once and for all at the creation. Rather, humanity *becomes* the image of God through an historical process that moves toward an escha-tological goal. In effect, humanity as image of God is first realized in Jesus, through his obedience and his resurrection. The resur-rection of Jesus Christ reveals that the ultimate destiny of *all* believers is to be transformed into the image of the risen Lord and therefore fully to become images and likenesses of God. This is the eschatological goal toward which history leads.[17] Pannenberg goes further, stating that to become image and likeness of God through Jesus' obedience and resurrection is the destiny not only of believers but of all humanity.[18]

Pannenberg clarifies the historicity of the resurrection and articulates its significance for our understanding of human nature and destiny. He does not, however, adequately illumine the impor-tance of the resurrection for Christian social ethics. Nor does he call attention to the profound and intimate relationship between the resurrection and Christian mission. These important omissions are related to Pannenberg's negative attitude toward secular liberation movements, which leads him into a fundamentally conservative political stance. Pannenberg warns against misunderstanding the freedom that comes to humanity through the resurrection as "emancipation" in the secular sense.[19] While asserting and affirming that the resurrection has implications for all dimensions of human life, including economics and politics, Pannenberg is more concerned with warning against misunderstandings and misuses of the resurrection than with indicating positively what these implications might be. He focuses almost completely on the ontological and eschatological significance of the resurrection, neglecting its social significance.

The writings of Sobrino, Moltmann and Segundo compensate for this missing element in Pannenberg's discussion. Sobrino emphasizes that the New Testament proclaims not the resurrection of "someone," but of Jesus of Nazareth, the man crucified as rebel and blasphemer, the man "condemned, executed and abandoned."[20] In other words, Jesus' resurrection by God validated the life Jesus lived, the values he represented and served and the vision he proclaimed.[21] As we have seen, this is a vision of the poor being lifted up, the hungry being filled, the rich being sent empty away and the mighty being put down from their thrones. Although it is a highly conflictual and provocative vision, in the long run it sees enmities overcome, distances eliminated and divisions transcended. It is a vision of all things reconciled in justice and love into a single, undivided reality. It is this vision and the life of the one in whom it was realized that are affirmed by the resurrection.

Jesus' resurrection affirms and confirms his proclamation that the kingdom of God has come. Segundo notes that the words attributed to the resurrected Jesus of the Gospels "do not seem to suggest any new teaching. . . . Indeed they seem to point to a new level of comprehension achieved by his disciples with regard to things that they already knew and that somehow had to do with their own status and mission."[22] And he writes of the resurrection appearances described by the evangelist: "It is as if Jesus' original exhortation, 'The Kingdom of God has come, repent, believe this good news' is still reverberating, though admittedly on a new level."[23]

Jesus' resurrection validates the kingdom life he lived and to which he called his disciples. And what is that life? It is the life of those who do not store up treasures for themselves on earth, but share with their brothers and sisters, thereby accumulating treasures in heaven; who do not hate and seek to conquer or destroy their enemies but love them and seek to set them free; who do not condemn sinners, but forgive them and welcome them into the kingdom and the church as they themselves have been forgiven and welcomed. This is the life that God validated when he raised Jesus from the dead. Those who live this life are following Jesus' advice to seek first the kingdom of God and its justice. With Jesus, they are on a quest for this justice. Being as wise as serpents, they are aware of the oppressive powers of this world and are prepared for the sufferings that come to those whose lives, by the grace of God, embody kingdom justice. The resurrection reveals that, against appearances, it is this life that triumphs and brings blessings for all humanity and the entire cosmos. The resurrection reveals that God's justice ultimately triumphs not through law, but through grace, which is another name for that Love which is God. The resurrection of Jesus from the dead is the most dramatic expression of this grace and love. It is also the greatest threat to the rulers of this age because it once and for all "puts the mighty down from their thrones." For this reason the rulers of this world can be expected to discredit or persecute those in whom resurrection life is manifest.

Both Moltmann and Sobrino emphasize the relationship between Jesus' resurrection and Christian mission. For Moltmann, there can be no unpartisan knowledge of Jesus' resurrection established on some objective basis, but only a knowledge that engages, claims allegiance and calls to missionary action.[24] In this respect, the resurrection appearances are like the calls of the prophets (see Isaiah 6; Ezekiel 1). The point of the call is not the vision itself or even the words, but the sending of the prophet on a mission for God. In his appearances to the disciples, the risen Jesus showed himself to them as alive, reaffirmed the call they had received from him, gave to this call a heightened eschatological urgency and sent them out in the power of the Spirit (John 20) or promised them that this power would come upon them (Luke 24).

Sobrino explains the reason for this relationship between resurrection and mission: "The historical aspect of Jesus' resurrection is to be grasped insofar as we see it in terms of a promise that opens up a future."[25] The resurrection as a promise regarding the future "provides the foundation for a universal hope that is capable of renewing the world and that is therefore necessarily bound up with the risk of faith."[26] Taking this risk of faith means engaging in Christian mission. This mission, however, is not to be understood in ecclesiastical terms—as recruiting people for the church and getting them to heaven. Christian mission is, in communion with the risen Jesus and his Spirit, proclaiming God's unconditional love, calling people to faith and inviting them to live by faith through participation in God's work of transfiguring the world so that it may reflect more perfectly the vision of the kingdom proclaimed by Jesus. The resurrection creates and sets in motion a community devoted to the implementation "in reality of those eschatological ideals of justice, peace and human solidarity"[27] that gave shape to Jesus' life. Faith in the resurrection of Jesus is best expressed in the lives of those believers who, in Jesus' name and for Jesus' sake, give themselves in the service of Jesus' vision. Through engagement in transformational praxis, such believers may come to comprehend and experience ever more deeply the meaning and power of Jesus' resurrection.

7

THE PASCHAL MYSTERY
AS REVELATION
OF GOD

The emphasis on the life and ministry of the historical Jesus
in chapter 5 is justified as a way of compensating for and comple-
menting the long preoccupation in Christian worship, piety, doctrine and theology with Jesus' death and resurrection. Any understanding of God and of Christian faith that ignores the significance
of the life and ministry of the historical Jesus inevitably will be
defective at best and heretical at worst. On the other hand, the
importance of Jesus' crucifixion and resurrection for our understanding of God and faith can scarcely be overemphasized. The
paschal event transforms Jesus' story into a radical new revelation
of God and of God's creation and its future and invests it with
cosmic meaning. Through faith, Christians participate in this paschal mystery liturgically, spiritually, ethically and politically. In the
power of the Spirit they are able to share in Jesus' experience and
knowledge of God as well as in Jesus' mission to the world.

New Knowledge of God through Jesus

Already during Jesus' earthly life, the community that surrounded him became aware that Jesus and the God he made
known could not be fully explained in terms of previous human
experience or existing religious categories. But only the climax of

Jesus' story, the paschal event, revealed the extent to which humanity's experience with Jesus transcended the limits of previous human experience of God and challenged the dominant human perceptions of reality.

The crucifixion and resurrection of Jesus set in motion a process of intellectual and theological reflection that led to a deeper understanding of who Jesus was and eventually to a new and revolutionary understanding of God. At the beginning of Part Two I suggested that the Christian understanding of God would be the foundation for the theology of peace and justice I hoped to develop. Now, in this concluding chapter, I want to talk more about this understanding in its most mature and developed form.

Let us begin by considering how this new understanding of God came about. Fundamentally it was the result of the community's reflection on its experience with Jesus.[1] In light of the extraordinarily radical nature of Jesus' life and teaching and the even more radical nature of his crucifixion and resurrection, the faith community was led to reflect for centuries in a very intense way on the question, Who is this Jesus? In the process of these reflections, the community discovered that this question was inextricably connected with an even more ultimate question: Who is the God Jesus points to and reveals and whose kingdom he proclaims and initiates on earth? During this period of intense theological reflection, the church defined who it understood Jesus to be and also arrived at the new and revolutionary understanding of God expressed in the doctrine of the Trinity.[2]

The process of reflection that led to the christological and trinitarian doctrine of the church was not solely intellectual; it was the result of the community's lived experience with Jesus. Crucial in this experience was the life of prayer—both personal and corporate—as well as the role of the Eucharist in the life of the community. Equally important were the ethical and political struggles with society that the community was involved in as a result of its efforts to remain faithful to Jesus as it understood him. Faithfulness was often perceived by the community as requiring costly resistance to the Roman world view and system, even in the period after Constantine. The theologies of such great church fathers as Irenaeus,

Origen, Athanasius and the Cappadocians and the doctrinal results to which they led cannot be properly understood apart from the spiritual, ethical and political struggles that the community was involved in, which created the context within which their theologies were articulated. These theologies were what liberation theologians say all theology must be, the result of critical reflection on lived experience in the world (praxis). Moreover, a definitive dimension of the experience on which these theologians reflected was the church's struggle to realize the true and full liberation of humanity.

What is the meaning of the controversies about who Jesus is? To what conclusions did they lead? Although focused on the question of the relationship between God and Jesus, these controversies address the larger question of the nature of the relationship between God and humanity and, by implication, between God and all material creation. They seek to articulate a proper understanding of the relationship between God and world, Creator and creation.

The Creator and Creation

Throughout these controversies about the relationship between God and Jesus, the point has been to avoid two diametrically opposed positions. On the one hand, creation in general and humanity in particular are not to be identified with God (pantheism). On the other hand, humanity and all material creation are not to be separated from or opposed to God (dualism).[3] On the contrary, through the incarnation all distance and separation between God and creation are to be seen as overcome. All creation, material as well as spiritual, is to be understood as existing in a relationship of inexpressible intimacy with God, in an eternal communion with God that not even death can dissolve. In the christological and trinitarian doctrines, God is portrayed as assuming the true humanity of Jesus within the person or hypostasis of the divine Logos. Henceforth, the humanity of Jesus precisely as humanity—that is, as creatureliness and as bodiliness—is destined to participate eternally in the fullness of the divine community's life. But Jesus is portrayed as the firstborn of many brothers and sisters. The sharing of the human being Jesus in the life of the divine community prefigures the ultimate destiny of all humanity and indeed all material creation.

The Christology of the councils, from Nicaea through Chalcedon, seeks to portray the nature of creation's sharing in the divine life in a particular way. According to this Christology, the true humanity in Jesus is not obliterated when assumed by the divine Logos, but *fulfilled*. The eschatological implication of this Christology is that at its consummation all creation will be taken up into the divine life in just such a way. The destiny of all creation, material and spiritual, is not to be merged with or obliterated by God but, freed from its bondage to corruption, to enjoy eternal communion with God the Creator. Just as the three divine persons retain their unique identities within the divine community, so Jesus and then all creation, while remaining distinct from God, exist eternally within God. Christian trinitarian and christological doctrines present a third alternative between pantheism and dualism. They define ultimate reality, which exists in and of itself and from and in which all else exists, as a triune Community that is nevertheless one Being.[4] And they understand all created reality as destined to participate eternally in the life of the one, triune God. Matthew Fox and others often refer to this vision as *panentheism*.

The Resurrection as Liberation

Although the whole of the original disciples' experience with Jesus was the origin and focus of this long process of theological reflection, the experience of the resurrection was of crucial significance. This unprecedented event shed light backwards on the experience of the disciples with the historical Jesus and, indeed, on the whole history of Israel. It also shed light forward into the future. In the Scriptures, the resurrection is understood as the event that reveals the future in store for believers and the whole created universe. That future will be determined not by entropy but by resurrection. In the resurrection of Jesus, the freeing of all material creation has already begun. The resurrection of Jesus from the dead is therefore seen as the ultimate liberation from death, sin and fear and as the beginning of that process through which God assumes creation into God's self while enabling it to remain creation.

Baptism and the Eucharist are tangible sacramental witnesses to the redemptive process through which all material reality is taken up into the divine life. In Baptism and the Eucharist, divine or resurrection life is communicated *through* material creation *to* material creation. The sacraments symbolize and prefigure the transfiguration of the whole material universe.

The Triune God of Love

The result of the long and intense process of theological reflection initiated by the faith community's experience of Jesus, especially his resurrection, was a new and revolutionary understanding of God,[5] namely, the understanding of God as triunity of Lover, Beloved and Love itself.

Moltmann believes that the emergence of the doctrine of the Trinity is closely related to the experience of God as Love. As stated in chapter 4, this experience was not new with Christianity but was a part of Israel's experience and faith. In Jesus, however, the experience of God as Love appears to have been deepened and radicalized. This radicalized experience of God as Love is expressed throughout the New Testament but its most succinct expression is in 1 John 4:16, where the apostle writes, "God is love."

Moltmann suggests that this awareness of God as Love led the faith community to conclude that traditional monotheism could not adequately express the richness of its experience of God. Rather, God must be understood as unity in plurality, plurality in unity. Moltmann traces the logic of that process in his book *The Trinity and the Kingdom.* He points out that the Christian tradition has always understood the confession "God is love" to be not only an assertion about the way God relates to the world but also about the innermost nature of God's divine being and life. As Moltmann puts it, "God not only loves, but *is* love."[6]

Traditional Jewish or philosophical monotheism could not express the richness of the mystery of the God who is Love because in human experience "love cannot be consummated by a solitary subject. An individuality cannot communicate itself; individuality

is ineffable, unutterable."[7] If God is Love, God must be conceived
as a community of interpersonal or suprapersonal Being. Following
this logic, the church in fact came to experience and confess God
as a Triunity of Lover, Beloved and Love itself. According to
Moltmann, it is this experience of God as plurality in unity, as
threeness in oneness, as divine community of persons, expressed
by the church in the doctrine of the Trinity, that makes the Christian understanding of God unique and revolutionary. Moltmann
points to Andrei Rublev's wonderful fifteenth-century icon of the
Trinity as perhaps the best visual representation of this doctrine.

> Through their tenderly intimate inclination towards one
> another, the three Persons show the profound unity joining
> them, in which they are one. As the chalice stands at the
> centre of the table round which the three Persons are sitting,
> so the cross of the Son stands from eternity in the centre of
> the Trinity. Anyone who grasps the truth of this picture under-
> stands that it is only in the unity with one another which
> springs from the self-giving of the Son (for many) that men
> and women are in conformity with the triune God.[8]

Creation as an Expression of God's Love

I already spoke briefly about the emergence in the faith of
Israel of belief in Yahweh as the creator God. The understanding
of God as divine community of Lover, Beloved and Love itself
made possible a further development of the scriptural theology of
creation as well as a deeper understanding of the relationship
between creation and redemption as the one, ongoing work of
God. Faith in the triune God and contemplation of this God's nature
and work lead also to a more profound awareness of the goodness
of creation. The Christian God *is* Love. A Christian understanding
of creation must be related to this experience of God as Love. God
creates because God is Love. And, as Moltmann says, in creating
God does not merely clone God's self but creates the true "other"
as dialogue partner, object of God's love and subject capable of
responding freely to love with love. Creation from this perspective is seen as an overflowing of God's love outside of God's self.
Moltmann writes, "It is in accordance with the love which *is* God
that God should fashion a creation which God rejoices over and
call to life God's Other, the human being, as God's image who

responds to God. Not to do this would contradict the love which God is. In the love which God is already lies the energy which leads God out of God's self and in the energy the *longing*, to use Berdyaev's words. Love does not permit the Lover to rest within himself. It draws him out of himself so that he may be entirely in the Beloved."[9] Christian faith therefore views creation as "a part of the eternal love affair between Father and Son. It springs from the Father's love of the Son and is redeemed by the answering love of the Son for the Father."[10]

Gerard Manley Hopkins captures this vision of creation as sacrament of God's love and as a part of the love affair between Lover and Beloved and expresses it in his great poem, "God's Grandeur."

> The world is charged with the grandeur of God.
> It will flame out, like shining from shook foil;
> It gathers to a greatness, like the ooze of oil
> Crushed. Why do men then now not reck his rod?
> Generations have trod, have trod, have trod;
> And all is seared with trade; bleared, smeared with toil;
> And wears man's smudge and shares man's smell: the soil
> Is bare now, nor can foot feel, being shod.
>
> And for all this, nature is never spent;
> There lives the dearest freshness deep down things;
> And though the last lights off the black West went
> Oh, morning, at the brown brink eastward, springs—
> Because the Holy Ghost over the bent
> World broods, with warm breast and with ah! bright wings.[11]

The obvious implication of this very high view of the goodness of creation, grounded in God's love, is that Christians are called to what might be described as a cosmic stewardship. This calling is already symbolized in God's commission to Adam to care for the Garden of Eden, but in light of a Christian understanding of creation it takes on new, more radical dimensions. And, considering the massive modern technologies, it also takes on new urgency. The first step in cosmic stewardship today is to work for peace and disarmament so as to remove the threat to creation presented by modern weaponry. It is *not* the vocation of humanity to uncreate all that God brought forth—to return the earth to the formless and chaotic darkness out of which God called it. Yet this is precisely the possibility that confronts us. Cosmic stewardship also requires us to participate in the struggle for justice in society and for justice in the relationship between humanity and nature.[12]

The Economy of Salvation

The Christian understanding of redemption also comes ultimately to rest in the Christian imagery of God as triune community of Lover, Beloved and Love itself. The central symbol of redemption in the Christian faith is the cross. The cross is the symbol through which all our theological and religious images must pass and is intimately connected to Christian faith's understanding of God as Love. The cross of Jesus points to the profound and inseparable relationship between love and suffering in the life of the divine Trinity and in Christian and human life in general. The cross reveals to us that the God who loves is the God who suffers. "If God were incapable of suffering, then he would be incapable of love or capable only of loving himself," says Moltmann. But if God is capable of loving something other than God, then "God lays Godself open to the suffering which love for another who is not self brings."[13] At the center of the Christian faith stands this image of the suffering God who loves human beings in their flesh and blood and in their sinfulness. This love is what leads God into suffering for the sake of and at the hands of God's beloved people, who reject, spurn and crucify the Lover. This poignant awareness of the suffering love of God appears already in certain passages in the Old Testament, as Terence Fretheim points out in his book *The Suffering of God*. Modern Jewish scholars such as Abraham Heschel and Martin Buber have also called attention to this. But it is in the passion of Jesus, the crucified Messiah, that the world is confronted with the scandal of the God who suffers because God loves in the most radical way.[14]

The New Testament constructs its economy of salvation on the basis of the cross and the suffering love of the triune God that it reveals. The Christian doctrine of redemption, mysterious and paradoxical as it may seem, insists that this suffering love of God, precisely through its vulnerability and apparent weakness, is the energy that overcomes sin, overthrows evil and draws the whole cosmos and all its inhabitants up into the life of the life-giving God.

This cosmic transfiguration effected through suffering love is the work of the Holy Spirit, who through the death and resurrection of Jesus is poured out on the world and whose transfiguring powers are renewing the face of the earth.[15] This belief in salvation through the cross, that is, through the suffering and dying love of God and God's people, appears absurd to those who do not believe and to those parts of believers' hearts that remain unbelieving. But to the eyes of faith the power of suffering love to overcome evil, achieve justice and transfigure all things is revealed. Paul speaks of this power in 1 Corinthians:

> The language of the cross may be illogical to those who are not on the way to salvation, but those of us who are on the way see it as God's power to save. As scripture says, "I shall destroy the wisdom of the wise and bring to nothing all the learning of the learned." Where are the philosophers now? Where are the scribes? Where are any of our thinkers today? Do you see now how God has shown up the foolishness of human wisdom? If it was God's wisdom that human wisdom should not know God, it is because God wanted to save those who have faith through the foolishness of the message that we preach. And so while the Jews demand miracles and the Greeks look for wisdom; here are we, preaching a crucified Christ, to the Jews an obstacle that they cannot get over, to the pagans, madness, but to those who have been called, whether they are Jews or Greeks, a Christ who is the power and wisdom of God. For God's foolishness is wiser than human wisdom and God's weakness is stronger than human strength. (1:18-25, Jerusalem Bible)

Dietrich Bonhoeffer, reflecting on this paradox of the cross in a section of his *Ethics* titled "Ecce Homo," wrote, "The figure of the crucified invalidates all thought which takes success as its standard."[16] It is not through power as the world knows it, not through wealth or weapons, that evil is overthrown and God's kingdom comes. Rather it is through the power of suffering love to persist in resisting exploitation, oppression, lies, violence and injustice. Those who practice this love—the prophets, apostles and martyrs of all ages—are united with Jesus and in the Spirit participate in the victory of his resurrection. No weapons and not even death itself can overcome the power of such love because it is stronger than death. Though all historical events are ambiguous signs at best,

Christians may, and probably should find it difficult not to ask themselves whether or not the remarkable and surprising changes in Eastern Europe and the Soviet Union in 1989, accomplished with remarkably little violence, could in part be a manifestation of the power of suffering love. This question comes all the more vigorously to the fore as one ponders the role of Christians in these events.

From the standpoint of worldly wisdom—the wisdom of the boardroom or the command center—this logic of the cross is truly madness. Tertullian, that clever second-century Christian lawyer, turned this apparent absurdity of faith in a crucified God into an argument in behalf of that faith. "Credo *ut* absurdum," he said, I believe because it is absurd—too absurd to have been thought up by human wisdom; therefore it must have been revealed by God.

Paul says that the cross, which is God's foolishness, has brought to naught human wisdom. The overwhelming problems that threaten the very existence of humanity on earth, which I discussed in Part One of this book, give new meaning to Paul's words. Human wisdom unguided by divine light created these problems, which now threaten humanity with extinction. This human wisdom proves each day its inability to solve the problems it has created. The more such wisdom accomplishes, the more problems we face. This wisdom is itself the problem.

Surely there must be something wiser than the wisdom that has led the world to the brink of extinction, subjected ever-increasing numbers to poverty and starvation while enriching an elite few, and deprived millions of their basic human rights in the name of communist or anti-communist ideologies. Paul tells us that this wiser thing is the wisdom of the cross, which reveals a God who, being Love, is vulnerable and who overcomes evil through suffering, sacrifice and what looks to the world like foolishness and weakness. God calls the people of faith, the Christian community, to live by this wisdom and to trust in it.

It may be difficult to see how the power of love, released in the sufferings of Jesus and his people, can overcome evil and save the world. Trust in the power of the bomb or the dollar may appear more sensible than trust in the cross, especially when it comes to worldly affairs. In fact, however, such expressions of power are destructive, satanic idols that, while promising life and salvation, in the end offer only death and destruction to the world. There is no common ground between this pagan trust in the power of human ingenuity and resources and trust in the power of the God of Love revealed in Jesus and incarnated in the world through the Spirit. The fulcrum time before which humanity stands requires a choice between a nihilistic god of power, death and violence who leads the world into the abyss of annihilation and the God of Love who creates something where there was nothing, raises the dead, forgives and reconciles sinners with God and one another and transfigures the whole created universe.

The Eschatology of Cosmic Redemption

The cross reveals that God redeems the world through the power of suffering love. The Christian doctrines of incarnation and resurrection of the body point to the fact that the object of the triune God's redemptive love is the entire universe that God created.

Too often Christian salvation is conceived in narrowly and exclusively spiritualistic or individualistic terms. In this view, through enlightenment by faith, the believer is snatched up out of this veil of tears and initiated into a hidden, inner, spiritual reality. This is a gnostic view of salvation that corresponds to the gnostic view of creation I spoke of earlier. Salvation is understood as salvation *from* rather than *of* the world. I believe Russian Orthodox philosopher and theologian Nicholas Berdyaev was right when, in reaction to this kind of theology, he declared that Christianity must be understood "not only as the religion of salvation but also of creativity, as the religion of the transfiguration of the world, universal resurrection, love toward God and human beings, a religion to be understood in terms of the entire content of the Christian truth about the coming Kingdom of God."[17] This affirmation of the cosmic dimension of redemption implies an eschatology of cosmic transfiguration. The foundation of this eschatology is the belief in the resurrection of Jesus from the dead and the Christian doctrine of the resurrection of the body, to which faith in Jesus' resurrection inevitably leads. For Christian faith, the end in store for the entire material universe is prefigured in the resurrection of Jesus, which is a work of and revelation of the triune God.[18]

The resurrection of Jesus is perceived in the New Testament not as an isolated event but as a critical threshold in the process by which the entire material universe is being transfigured. Through the resurrection of Jesus, the creation is liberated from the tyranny of the powers and principalities, both worldly and otherworldly. To be sure, the resurrection process has only just begun, but on the basis of the hope awakened at Easter, the whole creation waits and longs to be set free from its bondage to decay and obtain the glorious liberty of the children of God (see Rom. 8:18-25).

The consummation of this eschatological vision is the work of the Holy Spirit. The journey of the Son, whom the Father sends, through his life, suffering, death, and resurrection results in the outpouring of the Spirit. The eschatological work of the life-giving Spirit is, according to Moltmann, "physical resurrection, physical transfiguration and transformation of the physical form of existence."[19] The community of faith, made up of those who have received the Spirit through Baptism, accepted it in faith, and nourished it through the Eucharist, the word and prayer, participates in the Spirit's eschatological work of cosmic transfiguration and resurrection.

THE TRIUNE GOD AND THE
SHALOM KINGDOM

Why all this reflection on the fundamental doctrines of Christian faith—on God and Jesus and creation and salvation—in a book that attempts to develop a theology of peace and justice? I want to show that the struggle for justice and peace—or to use the more comprehensive biblical term, *shalom*—is not an optional or peripheral matter for Christian faith. It is a central and constitutive part of that faith. The most fundamental beliefs of Christian faith compel believers to participate in the struggle to establish *shalom* on earth because biblical faith is a lived relationship with the triune God who creates, redeems and transfigures the whole created universe in accord with God's nature as Love. As Bonhoeffer said, "Only those who obey, believe."[20]

Faith in the God of Love, whose will is the liberation of all things from their bondage to fear, death, sin and every other form of oppression, is a devastating criticism of all religion that is based on fear and that legitimates or even tolerates the demeaning exploitation or oppression of human beings or of nature. Such a faith requires believers to struggle against religion of this sort and also puts believers at odds with all social systems and policies that are demeaning, exploitive, alienating or oppressive. To the extent that the believing community lives its faith, it is at war with such systems and policies. The believing community's faith compels it to reject and resist a political system that perpetuates the division of humanity into "friend" and "enemy" on the basis of ideology. Faith in the triune God compels the Christian community to oppose a political policy based on the belief that peace and security can be achieved through the power of weapons capable of annihilating the "enemy." Faith in the God of Love cannot tolerate an economic system that allows or even encourages the privileged few to accumulate an abundance of the earth's resources while the many lack the most fundamental necessities of life. The faithful are obliged to fight against such a system and against the policies that enable it to survive. Faith in the triune God, who "transcends being God alone and lives in communion and friendship with creatures,"[21] is incompatible with tolerance of hierarchical and elitist social systems that deny people their human rights and oppress and enslave them economically, culturally, politically, religiously, sexually or in any other way. Rather, the form of social life consistent with faith in the triune God "is a universal community marked by justice and friendship; the end of such a community is the destruction of oppression and alienation and the achievement of full life for all creatures in God."[22]

Moltmann articulates the critique of oppressive authoritarian and patriarchal social systems implicit in trinitarian faith. He writes, "When the doctrine of the trinity vanquishes the monotheistic notion of the great universal monarch in heaven and the divine patriarch in the world . . . earthly rulers, dictators and tyrants [will] cease to find justifying religious archetypes."[23] The Christian doctrine of the Trinity unites the Almighty Father with Jesus, the crucified Son, and with the life-giving Spirit, who creates the new heaven and the new earth. According to Moltmann, "It is impossible to form the figure of the omnipotent, universal monarch, who is reflected in earthly rulers, out of the unity of *this* Father, *this* Son and *this* Spirit."[24] Moltmann considers what options in the political life of the human community would best reflect this Christian image of God as triune community of Lover, Beloved and Love itself. He concludes that the political option that best reflects on earth the life of the Divine Trinity is a "community of men and women, without privileges and without subjugation. The three divine Persons have everything in common, except their personal characteristics. So the Trinity corresponds to a community in which people are defined by their relations with one another and in their significance for one another, not in opposition to one another in terms of power and possessions."[25] Faith in the triune God compels Christians to strive for the realization of this vision not through repression and conformity but through a politics of love, freedom and creativity.

Faith in the triune God engages believers in the struggle to overthrow every form of oppression and exploitation and overcome all alienation because it awakens in them hope that a new heaven and a new earth in which every human being and all creatures are fully alive *can* and ultimately *will* become a reality. And faith enables believers to perceive their participation in this struggle for the new heaven and earth as a way of worshiping and serving and glorifying the triune God, because this is the sort of world God wills and this is the worship and service which pleases and glorifies God. It is worship in Spirit and in truth. As Irenaeus said, "The glory of God is a human being fully alive." When we work for conditions that allow all human beings to be fully alive, we glorify the philanthropic God of Jesus, the Father, the Son and the Holy Spirit.

British theologian Studdert Kennedy perceived and articulated the connection between faith in the Christian God and this struggle in his writings during World War I. Kennedy saw in the war a struggle between the God who through suffering love seeks to reconcile and heal the world and the god of pagan religions that seeks to impose its will on the world through violence and war. In his book *The Hardest Part*, Kennedy wrote, "I want to win the world to the worship of the patient, suffering, Father God revealed in Jesus Christ. . . . God, the Father of Love, is everywhere in history, but nowhere is He Almighty. Even and always we see him suffering, striving, crucified, but *conquering*. God is love."[26]

If this Christian doctrine and image of God as triune community of Lover, Beloved and Love itself replaces in our psyches, theologies and faith the pagan image of the inscrutable, exalted, imperial, macho Almighty Father, then our understanding of the mission of the church will be radically altered, as will our politics, economics, language and, indeed, our whole lives. Such altered consciousness and behavior on the part of a majority of the ecclesial community could effect dramatic change in the world, as the impact of individuals like Martin Luther King, Jr., Mahatma Gandhi, Desmond Tutu, Dorothy Day, Dom Helder Camara, Eivind Berggrav and others has shown.

Such a venturing forth in faith on the part of the whole people of God would be a major force for the emergence of a new world order that reflects more fully the reign of the Father, the Son and the Holy Spirit on earth. I believe that to embark more boldly on this venture is the calling and mission of the church in our day. My prayer is that the whole people of God may capture this vision of a transfigured world and work in the power of the Spirit to make that world a reality. Such a world will be very different from the one described in Part One of this book and will reflect much better the love of the triune God revealed to the world in Jesus of Nazareth.

NOTES

INTRODUCTION

1. Gerhard von Rad, "SHALOM," in *Theologisches Wörterbuch zum Neuen Testament*, ed. Gerhard Kittel (Stuttgart: Kohlhammer, 1950) 398–416.

CHAPTER 1.
SERPENTINE WISDOM IN AN AGE OF CRISIS

1. Remarks made in a paper given at a meeting of the International Studies Association, Washington, D.C., March 1985.

2. This is true not only of liberation theologians but of a wide spectrum of biblical and theological thinkers, including many evangelical theologians. The encyclicals and other writings and speeches of recent popes also express or imply support for the idea of Christianity's preferential option for the poor. See, for example, Pope John XXIII, *Mater et Magistra* (Glen Rock, N.J.: Paulist Press, 1961); Pope Paul VI, *Populorum Progressio* (Glen Rock, N.J.: Paulist Press, 1967); Pope John Paul II, *Addresses and Homilies Given in Brazil* (Washington, D.C.: U.S. Catholic Conference, 1980). In the latter, Pope John Paul II writes, "I rightly called for an option and preferences for the poor. . . . The poor are actually God's favorites."

3. According to Harold Sprout and Margaret Sprout (*Toward a Politics for the Planet Earth* [New York: D. Van Nostrand, 1971] 447), the

number of international organizations grew from less than 250 in 1910 to nearly 2,500 in 1970. Charles Chatfield, in his *Director's Manual for Wittenberg University's Geneva Program on Global Issues and the World Church* (unpublished), says that approximately 4,400 such organizations existed in 1986. A partial listing of these organizations is found on pp. 448–50 of the Sprouts' book and on p. 4 of the Brandt Commission's report, *North/South: A Program for Survival* (Cambridge: MIT Press, 1980).

4. Cf. Pierre Teilhard de Chardin, *The Phenomenon of Man* (New York: Harper & Brothers, 1959); idem, *Human Energy* (New York: Harcourt, Brace & World, 1969); Gerd Theissen, *Biblical Faith: An Evolutionary Perspective* (Philadelphia: Fortress Press, 1985).

5. Pierre Teilhard de Chardin, *Building the Earth* (London: Geoffrey Chapman, 1965); Theissen, *Biblical Faith*.

6. Cf. Jürgen Moltmann, *Theology of Hope* (New York: Harper & Row, 1967), especially his comparison of the world view of epiphany religions with that of religions of promise on pp. 95–102.

7. José P. Miranda contrasts Marxist and Christian hope in his book *Marx and the Bible* (Maryknoll, N.Y.: Orbis Books, 1974). His criticism of Marxism is not that it is too radical but that it is not radical enough because it is unable to affirm the resurrection of the dead. "What we must reproach Marx for when he avoids the problem of death, and therefore does not even glimpse the possibility of the resurrection of the dead is that he was not sufficiently dialectical" (p. 278).

8. Cf. Dietrich Bonhoeffer, *Ethics* (New York: Macmillan Co., 1955) 79–141.

9. The educational methodology of Brazilian educator Paulo Freire has played a significant role in helping Latin American peasants identify the social and political roots of their misery and organize to do something about it. See especially his *Pedagogy of the Oppressed* (New York: Herder & Herder, 1970).

10. Alvin Toffler, *The Third Wave* (New York: Bantam Books, 1980) 84–94. See also the excellent study by Henry Dobyns, *Native American Historical Demography* (Notre Dame: Indiana University Press, 1976), which examines the dramatic effects of European colonization on Native American population. According to one study cited by Dobyns (p. 4), the population of Central Mexico decreased from 16,800,000 in 1532 to 1,075,000 in 1605. The native populations in many Caribbean islands such as Trinidad and Tobago, small to begin with, often disappeared entirely. Dobyns's work includes an extensive bibliography of Native American historical demography.

11. Cf. Eugene D. Genovese, *The World the Slaveholders Made* (New York: Random House, 1969) esp. 3–20.

12. Simone de Beauvoir, *The Second Sex* (New York: Random House, 1974) xix ff., 160ff., 259ff. Male and female can also be associated with the dualism of mind and body. Cf. James B. Nelson, *Embodiment* (Minneapolis: Augsburg Publishing House, 1978) 58.

13. Nelson, *Embodiment*, 58.

14. Penny Lernoux, *The Cry of the People* (New York: Doubleday & Co., 1980). Discrimination and persecution in which religion plays a role linger on in places such as Northern Ireland, India and Sri Lanka. The recent riots between Christian Armenians and Muslim Azerbaijanis in the Soviet Union also show that religious loyalties are still capable of inspiring persecution and oppression.

15. Three well-known general surveys of the Holocaust are Lucy Davidowitz, *The War against the Jews* (New York: Bantam Books, 1976); Raoul Hilberg, *The Destruction of European Jewry* (New York: Harper & Row, 1979); and Martin Gilbert, *The Holocaust: The History of the Jews of Europe during the Second World War* (New York: Holt, Rinehart & Winston, 1985).

16. Examples of the growing liberation struggle can also be found in the work of many contemporary writers of fiction and poetry. Alice Walker is perhaps the best-known example, but the writings of Adrienne Rich, Ntozake Shange, Doris Lessing and Marilyn French, among many others, should be mentioned.

17. Sprout and Sprout, *Toward a Politics for the Planet Earth*, 402.

18. Toffler, *The Third Wave*, 319.

19. Richard J. Barnet and Ronald E. Muller, *Global Reach* (New York: Simon & Schuster, 1974) 256, 368–69.

20. Toffler, *The Third Wave*, 318.

21. Ibid., 317.

22. Mikhail Gorbachev has acknowledged and affirmed this fact in his public pronouncements and policies and most dramatically in his United Nations address in December 1988.

23. Toffler, *The Third Wave*, 318. Recent agreements to broadcast Soviet television programs in this country are a vivid example of the breakdown of psychological isolation, as is the Soviet Union's decision to stop jamming Voice of America broadcasts.

24. As far as I know, the term "humatriotism" originated with Dr. Theodore Lenz, one of the first American peace research scholars and the founder of a peace research institute in St. Louis, Missouri. Dr. Lenz created a questionnaire to test the level of a person's humatriotism.

25. Sprout and Sprout, *Toward a Politics for the Planet Earth*, 404–5.

26. Ibid., 405.

27. Ibid., 406.

28. Robert K. Merton, *Social Theory and Social Structure* (New York: Free Press, 1949) 79. Merton and other sociologists, such as Talcott Parsons, Theodor Newcomb, Edward Shils and Lewis Croser, also point out, however, that alternative social structures can be developed to fulfill the same function. Merton in particular emphasizes this point.

29. Ibid., 52.

30. The Chernobyl nuclear power plant accident of May 1986 is a dramatic example of this. Radioactive fallout from this accident was detected throughout most of the northern hemisphere. The deforestation of the slopes of the Himalayas by poor peasants seeking survival is another example. One result of that was a dramatic increase in flooding in Bangladesh. Examples such as this may be noted many times over.

31. Karl Marx, *Economic and Philosophic Manuscripts*, Manuscript One, quoted in *Writings of the Young Marx on Philosophy and Society*, ed. Lloyd Easton and Kurt Guddat (New York: Doubleday & Co., 1967) 293.

32. Cf. Elizabeth Dodson Gray, "Critique of Domination Theology," in Dieter T. Hessel, *For Creation's Sake* (Philadelphia: Geneva Press, 1985) 71–83; and Sallie McFague, *Models of God* (Philadelphia: Fortress Press, 1987) 59ff.

33. Missiologists call this relating of Christian faith to the experiential and cognitive worlds of non-Western cultures the process of "indiginization" or "contextualization."

34. A crass example of this in our own time is the preaching of such television evangelists as Jerry Falwell and Pat Robertson.

35. The best discussion of Bultmann's demythologization program is found in the series Kerygma und Mythos, ed. Hans Werner Bartsch (Hamburg: Reich & Heinrich, 1948–1964). Some of these articles are available in English in the series Kerygma and Myth (London: SPCK, 1953–1962).

36. Friedrich Engels's *Dialectics of Nature* was written from 1873 to 1886. Excerpts from this writing are included in the book *Marx and Engels on Religion* (New York: Schocken Books, 1964). The writings of Mexican exegete José P. Miranda attempt to bring together the insights of existentialism and Marx. See especially his *Being and the Messiah* (Maryknoll, N.Y.: Orbis Books, 1977).

37. Henri Bergson, *The Two Sources of Morality and Religion*, trans. R. Ashley Audra and Cloudesley Brereton (New York: Henry Holt & Co., 1935).

CHAPTER 2.
THE DYNAMICS OF UNDERDEVELOPMENT

1. These terms have become controversial in recent years, due to the impression that value judgments are associated with first, second

and third designations. The term "Third World" has been replaced in some quarters by the term "Two-thirds World." In most of what follows, the categories used will be "least-developed" and "less-developed" nations, referring to economic development.

2. Michael P. Todaro, *Economic Development in the Third World*, 3d ed. (New York and London: Longmans, Green & Co., 1984) 43.

3. Ibid., 31.

4. Bob Sabath, "The Bible and the Poor," *Post America* 3, no. 2 (1974): 73–75.

5. *North/South: A Program for Survival* (Cambridge: MIT Press, 1980) 32.

6. John Taylor, *Enough Is Enough* (London: SCM Press, 1975) 20.

7. Walter L. Owensby, *Economics for Prophets* (Grand Rapids: Wm. B. Eerdmans, 1988).

8. Tom Barry and Deb Preusch, *The Central America Fact Book* (New York: Grove Press, 1986) 140.

9. Ibid., 142.

10. Tom Barry, *El Salvador: A Country Guide* (Albuquerque, N.M.: The Inter-Hemispheric Education Resource Center, 1990) 177.

11. Ibid.

12. Ibid., 178.

13. Barry and Preusch, *The Central America Fact Book*, ix.

14. Todaro, *Economic Development*, 85.

15. Pope Paul VI, *Populorum Progressio* (Glen Rock, N.J.: Paulist Press, 1967) 38.

16. Many classical economists argue that, since growth can only be produced by capital that has been accumulated and then invested, the rich must be allowed to accumulate wealth to invest in development. Therefore, to limit this accumulation for the sake of equality of distribution is counterproductive. Todaro rejects this argument, at least for the Third World, for three reasons. First, the rich in Third World nations don't invest in Third World economies but squander their money on imported luxuries or put it in foreign banks. Second, Third World poverty results in physical and psychological handicaps that prevent large numbers of people from contributing to the productivity process and therefore to economic development. In order for development to get off the ground, the conditions of the masses must be improved so that a larger number of people can participate in the development process. Third, the bottom 40 to 60 percent of the people in many Third World nations are too poor to be consumers or to enter the modern sector of the economy in any way. Under these circumstances, the development process is severely constrained. Todaro concludes that development policies in the Third World must seek to equalize distribution of income as well as to promote growth if development efforts are to succeed.

17. Pope Paul VI, *Populorum Progressio*, 44.

18. See Todaro, *Economic Development*, 325–60, for a discussion of Third World education. Gandhi advocated and helped to establish an educational philosophy and practice in India similar to the one espoused by Todaro. Several Gandhian schools are still in existence in India today. Two of the best known are Gandhigram and Sevagram, both of which are pictured in the film *Gandhi's India* (London: BBC, 1969), available from Indiana University and other sources.

19. Todaro's *Economic Development*, chaps. 12–14, discusses problems of the international economic order. See also James McGinnis, *Bread and Justice* (Paramus, N.J.: Paulist/Newman Press, 1979) 55–324.

20. For an extensive and thoroughly documented account of economically motivated American political involvement throughout the Third World, see Noam Chomsky and Edward Herman, *The Washington Connection and Third World Fascism* (Boston: South End Press, 1979); and Penny Lernoux, *The Cry of the People* (New York: Doubleday & Co., 1980).

21. Dom Helder Camara makes these statements in an interview in the film *Excuse Me, America*, produced by the Catholic archdiocese of San Francisco, California, in 1979. Distributed by Phoenix Films, New York. This film, which includes interviews with Dorothy Day, Cesar Chavez and Mother Teresa, is available for distribution from many sources and is an excellent informative and inspirational documentary.

22. From 1983 to 1988 (and probably until the present, although data are not available) the net flow of resources was from the developing world to the developed world. In all but one of those years (1986) the volume of this flow increased, reaching $32.5 billion in 1988. See the chart "Reversing Financial Flows," prepared by the United Nations World Economic Survey and published by the United Nations Department of Public Information in 1989. From 1970 to 1990 the debt of the less- and least-developed countries increased from $58.1 billion to $990.3 billion. See the chart "Growing Mountain of Debt," prepared by the World Bank and published by the United Nations Department of Public Information in September 1989.

23. There is an excellent discussion of this issue in Mabub ul Haq, *The Poverty Curtain* (New York: Columbia University Press, 1976) 184–203. Ul Haq proposes the establishment of a world development authority, to be run by a board elected by the United Nations General Assembly, and the transformation of the International Monetary Fund into a true international central bank.

24. Philip Land, "A Comparative Survey of Significant Proposals for a New World Order," in *World Faiths and the New World Order*, ed. Joseph Gremillion and William Ryan (Interreligious Peace Colloquium, 1978) 4–47.

25. Pope Paul VI, *Populorum Progressio*, 62.

26. Quoted in Joseph Gremillion, *The Gospel of Peace and Justice* (Maryknoll, N.Y.: Orbis Books, 1976) 455–57.

27. Cf. Paulo Freire, *The Pedagogy of the Oppressed* (New York: Herder & Herder, 1970).

28. Chomsky and Herman, *The Washington Connection*, 45.

29. Jack Nelson Pallmeyer, *Hunger for Justice* (Maryknoll, N.Y.: Orbis Books, 1980) 61–62.

30. Chomsky and Herman, *The Washington Connection*, 49–50.

31. The filmstrip *Guess Who's Coming to Breakfast* (available through the Churches' Center for Corporate Responsibility, 475 Riverside Drive, New York, N.Y.) contains interesting graphic and documentary material on that coup.

32. The filmstrip *Sharing Global Resources* (available from NARMIC, a research group associated with the American Friends Service Committee, 1501 Cherry Street, Philadelphia, PA 19102) contains excellent graphs illustrating the destabilization program used to overthrow the Allende government.

33. Johan Galtung, "A Structural Theory of Imperialism," *Journal of Peace Research* 18, no. 2 (1971): 81–117.

CHAPTER 3.
THE NUCLEAR THREAT TO SURVIVAL

1. Edwin S. Schneidman, "Megadeath," in *Death and Dying, Challenge and Change*, ed. Robert Fulton (Boyd & Fraser, 1981) 376.

2. For a visual portrayal of the bombings of Hiroshima and Nagasaki, see the film *Hiroshima/Nagasaki* (New York: Museum of Modern Art, 1945), which is made up of scenes from the two cities taken by Japanese film crews on the days immediately following the bombing. It is available for purchase from the Metropolitan Museum of Art, New York, and from a number of agencies for rental. The films *The Last Epidemic* (Santa Cruz, Calif.: Impact Productions, 1980), produced by Physicians for Social Responsibility, and *The Lost Generation*, produced by the Lutheran Church of Japan in 1982, contain scenes from *Hiroshima/Nagasaki*.

3. The story "Sadako and the 1000 Paper Cranes" is a favorite among people in the peace movement. On a 1984 visit to the Soviet Union, I gave paper cranes made by the children in my daughter's elementary school in Sioux Falls, South Dakota, to Soviet schoolchildren in Novosibirsk, Siberia, and found that these children were very familiar with the story of Sadako.

4. Jonathan Schell, *The Fate of the Earth* (New York: Alfred A. Knopf, 1982) 11. Although the bomb itself weighed 8,000 pounds, the explo-

sive power of 12–15 tons of TNT was generated by converting one gram of matter to energy.

5. *A Sane Alternative* (Washington, D.C.: Students Against Nuclear Energy, 1985) 1–4. The distinction between tactical and strategic weapons is not always clear. Fundamentally, tactical weapons have lower megatonage, are incapable of traveling long distances, and are intended as artillery in battle. Strategic weapons are usually of greater megatonage and are targeted on and capable of reaching the enemy's home territory.

6. Most of this information comes from the *Defense Monitor* (1980), published by the Center for Defense Information, 122 Maryland Avenue, N.E., Washington, D.C. 20002; and from *The Last Epidemic*. The *Defense Monitor* is published several times a year and contains well-researched and updated information on weapons systems, including comparisons between American and Soviet systems.

7. From an article entitled "Feds Must Start Making Tough Budget Decisions," in the *Sioux Falls Argus Leader*, 5 Jan. 1987.

8. Information prepared by SANE, 711 G St., S.E., Washington, D.C. Source: Mid-season Review, Office of Management and Budget.

9. See the film *Hiroshima/Nagasaki*.

10. Ron Sider, *Nuclear Holocaust and Christian Hope* (Downer's Grove, Ill.: Intervarsity Press, 1982) 47.

11. Ibid., 37.

12. Jack Geiger, New York internist and epidemiologist, in the film *The Last Epidemic*.

13. *Long-term Effects of Multiple Nuclear Weapons Detonations* (Washington, D.C.: National Academy of Sciences, 1975). Quoted in Sider, *Nuclear Holocaust and Christian Hope*, 41–42.

14. Kosta Tsipis, *Physicians for Social Responsibility Newsletter*, December 1980, 3.

15. *Effects of Nuclear War* (Washington, D.C.: Office of Technology Assessment) 91.

16. Seymour Melman, *Pentagon Capitalism* (New York: McGraw-Hill, 1970); idem, *The Permanent War Economy* (New York: Simon & Schuster, 1974). Melman has researched the economic effects of high levels of military spending over long periods of time.

17. Melman, *Pentagon Capitalism*; idem, *Permanent War Economy*. See also Lloyd J. Dimas, "Economic Conversion, Productive Efficiency and Social Welfare," *Journal of Sociology and Social Welfare*, January–March 1977.

18. Melman, *Permanent War Economy*; idem, *The War Economy of the United States* (New York: St. Martin's Press, 1971); David Gold, et al., *Misguided Expenditures: An Analysis of the Proposed MX Missile System* (Council on Economic Priorities, 1987).

19. Gold, et al., *Misguided Expenditures*, 157.

20. Cf. Charles Lutz and Jerry Folk, *Peaceways* (Minneapolis: Augsburg Publishing House, 1983) 81–82.

21. Pope Paul VI, *Populorum Progressio* (Glen Rock, N.J.: Paulist Press, 1967) 76.

22. George H. Gallup, *The Gallup Poll: Public Opinion 1981* (Wilmington, Del.: Scholarly Resources, 1982) 163–65.

23. From an address by Jim Forest at a peace conference in Sioux Falls, South Dakota, October 1982.

24. Edwin S. Schneidman, "Megadeath," in *Death and Dying, Challenge and Change*, ed. Robert Fulton (Boston: Boyd & Fraser, 1981) 376.

25. Michael Mandelbaum, "The Bomb, Dread and Eternity," *International Security* 5, no. 2 (1980): 8–9.

26. Christopher Lasch, *The Culture of Narcissism: American Life in an Age of Diminished Expectations* (New York: W. W. Norton Co., 1978) 4.

27. Robert Lifton, *The Broken Connection* (New York: Simon & Schuster, 1979) 338.

28. Quoted in Rexford G. Tugwell, *A Chronicle of Jeopardy, 1945–1955* (Chicago: University of Chicago Press, 1955) 1.

29. In Edwin S. Schneidman, "Megadeath," 373. It seems to me that much contemporary art reflects an awareness of the omnipresence of megadeath. In popular art forms, especially the darker types of rock music, this awareness and the feelings of hopelessness, meaninglessness, resentment and anger which it generates are expressed.

30. Schneidman, "Megadeath," 372.

31. Ibid., 376.

32. Albert Einstein, *Einstein on Peace*, ed. Otto Nathan and Heinz Norden (New York: Avenal Books, 1981).

CHAPTER 4.
GOD AND ISRAEL

1. Chariton of Valamos, *The Art of Prayer: An Orthodox Anthology* (London, 1966) 184. Quoted by Colin Davey, "Anglicans and Eastern Christendom," *Sobornost* 7, no. 2 (1985): 14.

2. Karl Barth, *Fides Quaerens Intellectum* (London: SCM Press, 1960) 48. A little later, Barth writes, "[Anselm] prayed. God gave himself to know, and he was able to know God" (p. 170).

3. Jan van Ruysbroek, quoted in Maureen Conroy, "When I Am Weak, Then I Am Strong," *Contemplative Review*, Spring 1985, 36.

4. See the writings of Matthew Fox for a unique and intriguing understanding of spirituality that Fox refers to as "creation centered" and contrasts with "Fall/Redemption" spirituality. See especially his

Original Blessing (Santa Fe, N.M.: Bear & Co., 1983). See also Kenneth Leach, *Experiencing God: Theology and Spirituality* (New York: Harper & Row, 1985).

My appeal for an integrative theological methodology and emphasis on the role of prayer and spirituality in the theological task are not meant to deny or even minimize the importance of the speculative, metaphysical task of theology but to emphasize the importance of this task because it has been widely neglected by modern theology. With a few exceptions (process theology and neo-Thomism, for example), modern theology tends to understand Christian faith in terms of a biblically illumined human self-understanding (existentialism) or emphasizes the implications of the biblical understanding of God and God's will for the task of social reconstruction (liberation theology, theology of hope, political theology). Although these theologies have contributed greatly to our understanding of the faith for our time, I believe that neither human self-understandings nor theologically and biblically based social ethics can stand alone. Rather, they must be seen as integral parts of a total cosmic vision that rests ultimately on ontological and metaphysical premises. The credibility and power of Christian faith will be greatly enhanced if it can be interpreted in a way that is compatible with an intellectually responsible world view or can itself *inspire* such a world view. Therefore, theologians must take the risks involved in articulating an ontological and metaphysical world view inspired by the Christian faith but informed by knowledge of the physical, life, and social sciences. On the theoretical level, Gerd Theissen and Pierre Teilhard de Chardin have set their minds to that task. On the level of praxis, note that the political and ethical visions and actions of two of history's greatest social change agents, Mahatma Gandhi and Martin Luther King, Jr., were part of larger metaphysical visions, which no doubt contributed to the power and persistence of their movements.

The reflections of these modern thinkers and prophets suggest the possibility of a metaphysics of love that corresponds with the biblical description of God as love (1 John 4:16), which finds its ultimate expression in the doctrine of the Trinity. See Jürgen Moltmann, *The Kingdom and the Trinity* (New York: Harper & Row, 1981) 57ff.

5. Dietrich Bonhoeffer asks these same fundamental questions. See his *Letters and Papers from Prison* (New York: Macmillan Co., 1953) 279, 381.

6. See, for example, Ron Sider, *Nuclear Holocaust and Christian Hope* (Downer's Grove, Ill.: Intervarsity Press, 1982); idem, *Rich Christians in a Hungry World* (Downer's Grove, Ill.: Intervarsity Press, 1984).

7. Henry Englander, "The Exodus in the Bible," in *Studies in Jewish Literature*, ed. George Reimer (Berlin: G. Reimer, 1913) 108.

8. Ibid., 113.

9. Ibid., 115–16.

10. See, for example, the works of Walter Brueggemann, Jean Cardonnel, Jürgen Moltmann, Harvey Cox and Gustavo Gutiérrez.

11. Walter Brueggemann, *Living Toward a Vision* (New York: United Church Press, 1976) 56.

12. Jean Cardonnel, *L'Homme chretien et l'homme marxiste* (Paris and Geneva: La Palatine, 1964) 81.

13. François Biot, *Theologie de la politique* (Paris: Presses Universitaires, 1972) 129. Quoted in Norman Gottwald, *The Bible and Liberation* (Maryknoll, N.Y.: Orbis Books, 1984) 477–78.

14. Alfredo Fierro, "Exodus Event and Interpretation in Political Theologies," in *The Bible and Liberation*, ed. Norman K. Gottwald, 474–75.

15. Ibid., 479. Cf. José P. Miranda, *Marx and the Bible* (Maryknoll, N.Y.: Orbis Books, 1974).

16. Miranda (*Marx and the Bible*) points out that laws were originally called the *mishpatim* ("justices") of Yahweh. Miranda also argues that the purposes of Yahweh's *mishpatim* are to defend the weak, liberate the oppressed and see that justice is done for the poor. He also asserts, following Gerhard von Rad, that the adoption of these laws was originally connected with the liberation of the exodus, not with the Sinai tradition. "The observance of the laws," he says in reference to Psalm 105, "is not conceived as the human counterpart which responds to the divine beneficence, but rather as the last act of the great libertarian intervention with which Yahweh makes justice a reality. Everything is grace!" (p. 146). Miranda also observes that "unless justice is concretized in laws, the liberating intervention which Yahweh accomplished remains truncated" (p. 147). On the relationship between liberation as gift (exodus, gospel) and as task (justice), he concludes, "The most authentic and primordial theologization of the laws was made by connecting them with the characteristic essence of the God called Yahweh as he revealed himself when he broke into human history to save the oppressed from injustice" (p. 149).

17. This interrelationship between idolatry and injustice is the reverse side of the relationship between faith and justice, or, in the New Testament, between faith and love. Note, for example, Jesus' insistent linking of the two greatest commandments—love of God and love of one's fellow human beings.

18. Miranda, *Marx and the Bible*, 44.

19. Millard C. Lind, *Yahweh Is a Warrior* (Scottdale, Pa.: Herald Press, 1980) 169–70.

20. Ibid., 170.

21. Ibid., 171.

22. Ibid., 173. This prophetic criticism of ancient Near Eastern political religion and its role as an ideological support for the ruling nobility is certainly reminiscent of Marx's criticism of religion in the nineteenth century. Cf. *Writings of the Young Marx on Philosophy and Society*, ed. Lloyd D. Easton and Kurt Guddat (New York: Doubleday & Co., 1967) 250; and Karl Marx and Friedrich Engels, *On Religion* (New York: Schroder Books, 1964) 82–83, 145–49.

23. Much discussion has centered around the hardening of Pharaoh's heart in Exodus. Does Pharaoh harden his own heart or does God harden it? The story itself expresses the action both ways. See the excellent discussion of this subject in Brevard Childs, *The Book of Exodus: A Critical Theological Commentary* (Philadelphia: Westminster Press, 1974) 170–75. Childs concludes that the "polarity between hardening as a decision of Pharaoh and as an effect of God never was seen (by the author) as a major issue" (p. 174). Rather, says Childs, the hardening in Exodus is closely connected to the giving of signs and is a way of explaining how a series of divine signs could fail to achieve its purpose.

24. Terence Fretheim, *The Suffering of God* (Philadelphia: Fortress Press, 1984) 2.

25. "Love," in *Hastings Dictionary of the Bible*, ed. G. G. Findlay (New York: Charles Scribner's Sons, 1963) 593.

26. The theme of God's philanthropy is strongly emphasized in the Byzantine tradition. One of the beautiful parts of the *Liturgy of St. John Chrysostom* is the phrase with which the prayers close, "For you are gracious and the lover of humanity" *(philanthropos)*. This understanding of God as the ultimate humanist or philanthropist is underscored by St. Irenaeus's phrase, "The glory of God is a human being fully alive" *(Against Heresies* I.6.2).

27. Gerhard von Rad, *Old Testament Theology* (New York: Harper & Row, 1965) 1:146. I would add that, in a sense, the pattern in which all creation was fashioned is to be sought *outside* creation, that is, in God.

28. Lind, *Yahweh Is a Warrior*, 172.

29. Brueggemann, *Living Toward a Vision*, 93.

30. In what seems to me a shocking example of theological obtuseness, the editors of the Oxford Annotated Bible seek to elucidate this passage with the following comment: "Judah's limited treasure precluded extensive military expenditures. Her terrain was unfavorable for Egyptian chariots." As though the issues were economic or logistical rather than theological!

31. The Orthodox tradition seems to have maintained a keener sense of the unity between creation and redemption, largely because

of its emphasis on and interpretation of the future eschatological consummation. According to George Florovsky, "The resurrection of dead is the one and unique destiny of the *whole world*, of the *whole cosmos!*" (*Creation and Redemption* [Springfield, Va.: Norland Publishing Co., 1976] 130). See also Jürgen Moltmann, *God in Creation* (New York: Harper & Row, 1985). Russian philosopher Nicholas Berdyaev has reinforced this ancient insight of Eastern Christianity. See his article, "Salvation and Creativity: Two Understandings of Christianity," in *Two Roads of Western Spirituality*, ed. Matthew Fox (Santa Fe, N.M.: Bear & Co., 1980) 115–39. In the West, the poetic vision of Teilhard de Chardin has related it to the modern evolutionary perspective. See his *The Phenomenon of Man* (New York: Harper & Brothers, 1959).

32. A number of attempts are being made today to develop a holistic theology that sees God's work of creation, redemption and transformation as an organic unity. For an American pioneer in this effort, see Joseph Sittler, *The Ecology of Faith* (Philadelphia: Muhlenberg Press, 1961). The renewed interest in the theology of Irenaeus is a part of this effort to develop a holistic theology. See Gustav Wingren, *Man and the Incarnation* (Edinburgh: Oliver & Boyd, 1959); and Paul Santmire, *The Travail of Nature* (Philadelphia: Fortress Press, 1985). The writings of Matthew Fox, with their attempt to recover a creation-centered spirituality, are also of importance here. See Fox, *Original Blessing*; idem, *A Spirituality Named Compassion* (Minneapolis: Winston Press, 1979); idem, *Western Spirituality: Historical Roots, Ecumenical Routes* (Santa Fe, N.M.: Bear & Co., 1980); idem, *Breakthrough: Meister Eckhart's Creation Spirituality, A New Translation* (New York: Doubleday & Co., 1982).

33. Some biblical exegetes have pointed out that dominion, far from legitimating exploitation, entails stewardship or caretaking responsibilities. See James Limburg, "What Does It Mean to 'Have Dominion over the Earth,'" *Dialogue* 10, no. 3 (Summer 1971): 221–23. See also the excellent discussions on the relationship between God and nature in Santmire, *The Travail of Nature*, chap. 10; and Grace Jantzen, *God's World, God's Body* (Philadelphia: Westminster Press, 1984). These discussions of the biblical term "dominion" are sometimes a response to criticisms of environmentalists such as Ian McHarg, Ann Ehrlich, Paul Ehrlich and others, who blame the biblical theology of dominion for the arrogant and exploitive treatment of nature by modern, Western society.

34. Fox reflects on this relationship between justice in cosmos and community in his *Illuminations of Hildegard of Bingen* (Santa Fe, N.M.: Bear & Co., 1985) 45. He writes, "The universe itself works by laws of harmony and balance, that is, by way of justice. Justice is not a moral virtue, an ethical norm as humans conceive it, it is an operative pattern

by which the universe holds together and is symmetrically bound. . . . Humans are invited to enter the patterns which exist everywhere we look, including our own bodies." Fox quotes St. Hildegard, who wrote, "If we abuse our condition and commit evil deeds, God's justice will allow other creatures to punish us." Fox concludes, "The abuse of the land or the waters, the air or the atomic powers of the universe, will lead to the just punishment of the species that has heaped that abuse. Justice is not rained down from above by a vengeful God. Rather it comes from the web of creation itself."

35. Santmire, *The Travail of Nature*, 35–36. The theological tradition begun by Irenaeus is strong evidence that a theology that views creation, redemption and transformation as one ongoing, holistic process is not the product of modern theologians but enjoys a long history in Christianity. Aloys Grillmeyer states that for Irenaeus, "Creation, the incarnation of Christ, redemption, and the resurrection belong together as different parts of the one all-embracing saving work of God" (*From the Apostolic Age to Chalcedon* [New York and London: Sheed & Ward, 1965] 101).

CHAPTER 5.
JESUS, GOD AND THE KINGDOM

1. I use "religion" here as Dietrich Bonhoeffer does in *Letters and Papers from Prison* (New York: Macmillan Co., 1953) 279–82, 325–29, 360–69. According to Bonhoeffer, religion speaks of God at the edges of life, when human knowledge is exhausted. He would speak of God at the center. Religion speaks of God individualistically and metaphysically. Bonhoeffer would speak of God in a *worldly* sense, and of community and God.

2. "Religious suffering is the *expression* of real suffering and at the same time the *protest* against real suffering. Religion is the sigh of the oppressed creature, the heart of a heartless world, as it is the spirit of spiritless conditions. It is the opium of the people." Karl Marx, *Toward the Critique of Hegel's Philosophy of Law*. Quoted in *Writings of the Young Marx on Philosophy and Society*, ed. Lloyd Easton and Kurt Guddat (New York: Doubleday & Co., 1967) 250.

3. I have learned this from many people, but Ernst Käsemann was my most important teacher on this matter. Käsemann's passionate insistence on the uniqueness of Jesus and what I believe is Käsemann's love for Jesus impressed and inspired me deeply during my years as a student at Tübingen. Käsemann never tired of emphasizing the impossibility of using Jesus' message and vision for oppressive purposes. Cf. Käsemann, *Jesus Means Freedom* (Philadelphia: Fortress Press, 1969).

4. A number of New Testament scholars recently have pointed out that modern Christians can know more about the pre-ecclesial Jesus and his movement than any generation of Christians since the first century. Cf., e.g., Larry Rasmussen, "Jesus and the Moral Life," paper delivered at the Society of Christian Ethics meeting, Chicago, January 1986; James M. Robinson, *The New Quest for the Historical Jesus* (Philadelphia: Fortress Press, 1983); E. P. Sanders, *Jesus and Judaism* (Philadelphia: Fortress Press, 1985).

5. The work of Reimarus was published posthumously by the German author Gotthold Ephraim Lessing in 1788.

6. Albert Schweitzer, *The Quest of the Historical Jesus* (New York: Macmillan Co., 1956).

7. Ernst Käsemann, "Das Problem des historischen Jesus," *Zeitschrift zur Theologie und Kirche* 51 (1954): 125–53.

8. The work of C. G. Jung and his disciples is very important for understanding the place of religion and religious myths and dreams in the human psyche. Jung's view was that religion and religious mythology are of extreme importance in understanding the human psyche and in the psyche's quest for health but that the psychological dimension of religion cannot be made the basis for either affirming or denying the (objective) existence of the realities to which these myths point.

9. Rasmussen, "Jesus and the Moral Life," 2.

10. Norman Perrin, *Rediscovering the Teaching of Jesus* (London: SCM Press, 1967) 54.

11. John Dominic Crossan, *In Parables: The Challenge of the Historical Jesus* (New York: Harper & Row, 1973). Crossan's work has recently been criticized by James Breech in his study *Jesus and Postmodernism* (Philadelphia: Fortress Press, 1989). Breech claims that Crossan's interpretation of Jesus' parables is based on a hermeneutical presupposition that death is good. In my view, Breech fails to substantiate this claim and therefore his criticism of Crossan's work, which rests on his claim, is unconvincing. Breech does agree with Scott and Crossan that "Jesus' parables are utterly dissimilar from any other stories known in Hellenistic and Greco-Roman antiquity, including Rabbinic stories." According to Breech, "Jesus was the first narrator in the West to tell non-didactic, non-moralizing fictional realistic narratives." If this is true, Breech says, "it was also Jesus who first liberated the human imagination by communicating the truth about reality" (p. 64). These and numerous similar passages prove that there are many similarities between Breech's study and those of such New Testament scholars as Perrin, Scott and Crossan.

12. Bernard Brandon Scott, *Jesus: Symbol-Maker for the Kingdom* (Philadelphia: Fortress Press, 1981). See his discussion on pp. 5–18.

13. José P. Miranda, *Marx and the Bible* (Maryknoll, N.Y.: Orbis Books, 1974) 211–13. "To keep the *eschaton* perpetually in the future was precisely the recourse of Jewish stubbornness in order to reject Jesus Christ. And even today it is still the ironclad refuge of obduracy" (p. 212). Sanders makes a similar point in his book *Jesus and Judaism*, 90.

14. Scott, *Jesus: Symbol Maker for the Kingdom*, 155. Crossan describes the central significance of the parables in communicating Jesus' vision this way: "There is an intrinsic and inalienable bond between Jesus' experience and Jesus' parables. A sensitivity to the metaphorical language of religious experience and an empathy with the profound and mysterious linkage of such experience and such expression may help us to understand what is *most* important about Jesus: his experience of God" (*In Parables, The Challenge of the Historical Jesus* [New York: Harper & Row, 1973] 22).

15. Perrin, *Rediscovering the Teaching of Jesus*, 58–59.

16. I have adapted this from Scott, *Jesus: Symbol Maker for the Kingdom*, 13.

17. Crossan, *In Parables*, 63–64. This radical vision of the kingdom that overthrows the world is communicated in parable after parable. Speaking at a meeting of the American Academy of Religion several years ago about the Parable of the Pharisee and the Publican, Crossan gave another graphic example. He said that to grasp the effect this parable would have had on Jesus' audience, we should begin, "A pope and a pimp went into the temple to pray."

18. I once heard Gerhard Ebeling shed light on this relationship between form and content in the parables of Jesus. He pointed out that there is always a distance between language and the reality to which it points but that in Jesus' parables the language is so close to the reality as to almost be the reality itself.

19. Scott, *Jesus: Symbol-Maker for the Kingdom*, 109–12. This figure is adapted from several charts in Scott's book. Figure 3, p. 99 is from ibid., p. 120.

20. In the Old Testament and in many passages of the New Testament, leaven is a symbol of moral corruption. Cf. ibid., 75–77.

21. The category "comedy through tragedy," which Scott believes describes Jesus' view of the kingdom, contrasts with the popular opinion that sees the kingdom as comedy (i.e., an assurance of blessing) for the accepted and as tragedy for the enemies of the kingdom.

22. Crossan, *In Parables*, 32.

23. Sanders, *Jesus and Judaism*, 90.

24. André Trocme, *Non-Violent Revolution* (Scottdale, Pa.: Herald Press, 1973) 29; John Howard Yoder, *The Politics of Jesus* (Grand Rapids: Wm. B. Eerdmans, 1972) 34–37.

25. Gerd Theissen, *The Sociology of Early Palestinian Christianity* (Philadelphia: Fortress Press, 1977) 8–16.

26. Ibid., 17–23. This emphasis on the economic solidarity of the community continued to be strong in early Christianity and was often expressed in the sermons of the great church fathers. John Chrysostom's words in Homily 12 on 1 Timothy are representative of early church teaching on this subject: "The community (of goods) is far more suitable to us and is better grounded in nature than (private) property" (quoted in Dennis Guolet, *The Cruel Choice* [New York: Atheneum, 1978] 4–5).

27. Sanders, *Jesus and Judaism*, 164.

28. Juan Luis Segundo says that in Mark, which emphasizes the miracles of Jesus, only one miracle was performed for the benefit of someone who was not poor, namely, the raising of Jairus's daughter. See *The Historical Jesus of the Synoptics* (Maryknoll, N.Y.: Orbis Books, 1985) 211 n. 7.

29. Theissen, *Sociology of Early Palestinian Christianity*, 15.

30. Leonard Swidler, *Biblical Affirmations of Women* (Philadelphia: Westminster Press, 1979) 164. Swidler's book contains many more examples of stories of Jesus in which the full humanity of women is emphasized (see pp. 161–290).

31. Ibid., 173–78.

32. Ibid., 193.

33. Ibid., 172–73. It is interesting to note that Gandhi, who throughout his life was fascinated by Jesus, prided himself on being "half woman and half man" (Erik Erikson, *Gandhi's Truth* [New York: W. W. Norton, 1969]). I take this to mean that Gandhi was open in considerable measure to those sensitivities and experiences generally associated with the feminine. In terms of Jungian psychology, Gandhi was reconciled with his feminine side. This also appears to have been the case with Jesus.

34. Swidler, *Biblical Affirmations of Women*, 181–82.

35. Ibid., 180–81.

36. Ibid., 209–10.

37. Ibid., 203.

38. Cf. William Klassen, *Love of Enemies* (Philadelphia: Fortress Press, 1984) 72–109; J. Massingbaerde Ford, *The Enemy Is My Guest* (Maryknoll, N.Y.: Orbis Books, 1982); Ronald Sider and Richard Taylor, *Nuclear Holocaust and Christian Hope* (Downer's Grove, Ill.: Intervarsity Press, 1982); James B. Douglass, *The Non-Violent Cross* (New York: Macmillan Co., 1966) 3–78, 217–92; idem, *Contemplation and Resistance* (New York: Doubleday & Co., 1972) 79–108; Yoder, *The Politics of Jesus*; Trocme, *The Non-Violent Revolution*.

39. According to Klassen (*Love of Enemies*, 84), Rudolf Bultmann argued for the authenticity of this teaching as a word of Jesus because it was not found in the Judaism of his day. Klassen points out that since Bultmann the exhortation to love one's enemies has been found in the teaching of the rabbis but not in the same categorical form as in Jesus' teaching. On the basis of conversations with rabbis, I would risk saying also that this law of nonretaliation never played such a normative and central role in Judaism as it did in early pre-Constantinian Christianity. Thus, the importance of enemy love may have been one of the reasons Jewish Christians did not participate in the Jewish uprisings against Rome in the first and second centuries.

40. Ibid., 85.

41. Eduard Schweitzer, *The Good News According to Matthew* (Atlanta: John Knox Press, 1975) 194.

42. Klassen, *Love of Enemies*, 84.

43. Reinhold Niebuhr, *Why the Christian Church Is Not Pacifist* (London: SCM Press, 1940) 17. Reprinted in idem, *Christianity and Power Politics* (New York: Charles Scribner's Sons, 1940).

44. Reinhold Niebuhr, *An Interpretation of Christian Ethics* (reprint; New York: Harper & Row, 1979) 196.

45. Niebuhr, *Why the Christian Church Is Not Pacifist*, 16.

46. Segundo, *The Historical Jesus of the Synoptics*; G.H.C. MacGregor, *The New Testament Basis of Pacifism* (Nyack, N.Y.: Fellowship Publications, 1954); idem, *The Relevance of an Impossible Ideal* (Nyack, N.Y.: Fellowship Publications, 1954).

47. Luise Schottroff and Wolfgang Stegemann, *Jesus and the Hope of the Son* (Maryknoll, N.Y.: Orbis Books, 1986).

48. Quoted from Richard Taylor and Ronald Sider, "Fighting Fire with Water," *Sojourners* 12, no. 4 (April 1983): 16.

49. Cf. the beautiful biography of Gandhi by Stanley Jones, *Gandhi, Portrayal of a Friend* (Nashville: Abingdon, 1983).

50. Mahatma Gandhi, *Collected Works*, ed. K. Swaminathan and Ur Rao, vol. 51 (Chicago: Greenleaf Books, 1983) 145.

51. Erikson, *Gandhi's Truth*, 306.

52. Jones, *Gandhi, Portrayal of a Friend*, 151. For a study of Gandhi and nonviolence, see Gene Sharp, *Gandhi as a Political Strategist* (Boston: Porter Sargent, 1979); and idem, *Social Power and Political Freedom* (Boston: Porter Sargent, 1980). See also Joan Bondurant, *Conquest of Violence* (Berkeley and Los Angeles: University of California Press, 1971).

53. Cf. Roland Bainton, *Christian Attitudes toward War and Peace* (Nashville: Abingdon Press, 1960); G. J. Heering, S.J., *The Fall of Christianity* (Nyack, N.Y.: Fellowship Publications, 1943); C. F. Cadoux, *The Early Christian Attitude to War* (Headley Brothers, 1919); Macgregor, *The*

New Testament Basis of Pacifism; Charles P. Lutz and Jerry Folk, *Peace-ways* (Minneapolis: Augsburg Publishing House, 1983) 131–33; Jerry Folk, *Worldly Christians* (Minneapolis: Augsburg Publishing House, 1983) 101–3.

54. Richard Cassidy, *Jesus, Politics and Society* (Maryknoll, N.Y.: Orbis Books, 1978) 60.

55. Eric Fromm, *The Heart of Man* (New York: Harper & Row, 1964) 89.

56. Cassidy, *Jesus, Politics and Society*, 52, 61.

57. Juan Luis Segundo, *Faith and Ideology* (Maryknoll, N.Y.: Orbis Books, 1984).

58. Ibid., 42.

59. Ibid.

60. Jürgen Moltmann, *The Crucified God* (New York: Harper & Row, 1974) 129. Bonhoeffer's later writings about a religionless Christianity are relevant in connection with this discussion. See n. 1 of this chapter for references.

61. Segundo, *Faith and Ideology*, 471.

CHAPTER 6.
THE POLITICAL SIGNIFICANCE OF JESUS'
DEATH AND RESURRECTION

1. Jürgen Moltmann writes, "Anyone who preaches the imminent Kingdom of God not as judgement, but as the gospel of justification of sinners by grace and demonstrates it through his relationships with sinners and tax collectors contradicts the hope based upon law, is deceiving sinners and tax collectors and is blaspheming the God of hope. Clearly this drastic novelty and contradiction formed part of the preaching and the ministry of Jesus from the first" (*The Crucified God* [New York: Harper & Row, 1974] 129).

2. *Writings of the Young Marx on Philosophy and Society*, ed. Lloyd Easton and Kurt Guddat (New York: Doubleday & Co., 1967) 249.

3. Cf. Moltmann, *The Crucified God*, 128–45.

4. Ibid., 127.

5. Rudolf Bultmann, "The Primitive Christian Kerygma," in *The Historical Jesus and the Kerygmatic Christ*, ed. Carl Braaten and Roy Harrisville (New York and Nashville: Abingdon, 1964) 24. Cited by Moltmann in *The Crucified God*, 137.

6. Moltmann, *The Crucified God*, 137, 138.

7. Ibid., 138.

8. Ibid., 144. Moltmann follows this statement with a wonderful quotation from the second-century pagan opponent of Christianity, Celsus: "Since demons rule in the world, anyone who wishes to live there must show them veneration and submit to their ordinances. And

therefore one must also submit to rulers, even if they demand that one takes an oath in their name. Through this belief Rome grew great and it is not right to reject their gods and accept a God who is not even able to give their followers a patch of earth or a house so that they have to slink about secretly in constant fear."

9. Moltmann, *The Crucified God*, 138–39.

10. Oscar Cullmann, *The State in the New Testament* (New York: Charles Scribner's Sons, 1956); Moltmann, *The Crucified God*, 137–44; Jon Sobrino, *Christology at the Crossroads* (Maryknoll, N.Y.: Orbis Books, 1978) 211–13.

11. Moltmann, *The Crucified God*, 142.

12. Sobrino, *Christology at the Crossroads*, 214.

13. Ibid., 220–21.

14. Ibid., 229.

15. Cf. Moltmann, *The Crucified God*, 166–99; Sobrino, *Christology at the Crossroads*, 229–72; Wolfart Pannenberg, *Jesus, God and Man* (Philadelphia: Westminster Press, 1968) 53–114; Rudolph Schnachenberg and Wolfart Pannenberg, *Ostern und der neue Mensch* (Frankfurt: Herder, 1981); Gerald O'Collins, S.J., *The Resurrection of Jesus Christ* (Valley Forge, Pa.: Judson Press, 1973); Juan Luis Segundo, *The Historical Jesus of the Synoptics* (Maryknoll, N.Y.: Orbis Books, 1985) 166–77.

16. Pannenberg, *Jesus, God and Man*, 98.

17. Wolfart Pannenberg, *Auferstehung Jesus und Zukunft des Menschen* (Frankfurt: Herder, 1981) 57–59.

18. Ibid., 67–68. It is unfortunate that Pannenberg does not consider the implications of the resurrection for the cosmos as a whole. A discussion of the theme would have fit well in his section on the church as the present form of the future of Christ (pp. 78–83).

19. Ibid., 61.

20. Sobrino, *Christology at the Crossroads*, 243.

21. Segundo, *The Historical Jesus of the Synoptics*, 171.

22. Ibid., 169.

23. Ibid., 171.

24. Cf. Moltmann, *The Crucified God*, 172–73.

25. Sobrino, *Christology at the Crossroads*, 253.

26. Ibid., 253. Quoted in Jürgen Moltmann, *Hope and Planning* (New York: Harper & Row, 1971).

27. Sobrino, *Christology at the Crossroads*, 255.

CHAPTER 7.
THE PASCHAL MYSTERY AS REVELATION OF GOD

1. Alloys Grillmeyer writes, "At the beginning of (Christian) history stands the Christ-event, Christ's revelation, and, above all, Christ him-

self as a person. From the very beginning, an intellectual struggle set in over this event and this person which is to be counted among the most profound of all human controversies, within Christianity or outside it" (*Christ in Christian Tradition* [New York and London: Sheed & Ward, 1965] xxiii).

2. "The [doctrine of the] Trinity is the product of the wrestling of the earliest church with the question of the relation of Jesus to God" (Susan Thistlethwaite, "Violence and the Doctrine of God," the Georgia Harkness Lectures, lecture 1, 1984, p. 3).

3. Orthodox Christianity, especially in the West, to the extent that it has been identified with patriarchy, has no doubt emphasized the transcendence of God so exclusively as to nearly lose sight of God's imminence. Starhawk among others has called attention to this. She writes, "The conceptions of justice in Western patriarchal religions are based on a world view which located deity *outside* the world. . . . The major difference between patriarchal religions and the evolving goddess religions . . . is the world view that includes regarding divinity as imminent—as in the world, not outside the world" (in Charlene Spretnak, ed., *The Politics of Women's Spirituality* [New York: Doubleday & Co., 1982] 416).

4. Jon Sobrino (*Christology at the Crossroads* [Maryknoll, N.Y.: Orbis Books, 1978] 323–24) clarifies the relationship between revelatory historical events and doctrinal affirmations about ultimate reality by making a distinction between "historical" and "doxological" statements. The christological and trinitarian dogmas of the church are doxological affirmations, that is, statements that seek to formulate the mysterious reality of God in God's self. According to Sobrino, doxological statements of this sort "cannot be intuited in themselves; they are possible only on the basis of the historical statements." As doxological statements, christological and trinitarian formulations are reflective interpretations of the faith community's experience with Jesus developed within the context of the community's life of faith, itself lived in the midst of the world. These formulations draw conclusions about God in God's self that, although based on the community's historical experience with God in Jesus, go beyond this experience and cannot be proven by the experience. Rather, as doxological statements they seek to illumine *ultimate reality;* therefore, their affirmation requires a leap of faith. Those who make this affirmation experience a rupture in the reasoning process because doxological statements about God in God's self are beyond the ability of reason alone to grasp. Ultimate reality is always shrouded in mystery; doxological statements can only point to and illumine that mystery. To believe is ultimately to surrender to the mystery. According to Sobrino, therefore, the embracing of a doxological statement requires a "surrender of the ego on the rational level,

and . . . in real life." Indeed, in Sobrino's view, this surrender of the ego required for the affirmation of Christian dogma about ultimate reality is one of the important functions of dogma. Sobrino's understanding of the way doxological or dogmatic statements function is similar to the way some modern philosophers of science understand scientific hypotheses of the most comprehensive sort to function. Hypotheses such as Einstein's Theory of Relativity, though based on empirical evidence, go beyond the evidence in constructing a picture of reality as a whole. Therefore, the acceptance of these hypotheses requires a certain element of faith.

Grillmeyer makes a similar point in his book *Christ in Christian Tradition*. He points out that the christological heresies rejected by the church were attempts to rationalize, explain, control and thereby dissolve the mystery. The formulas adopted by the church, on the other hand, "represent the *lectio difficilior* (more difficult reading) of the gospel and maintain the demand for faith and the stumbling block which Christ puts before humanity" (p. 493). In other words, the christological and trinitarian formulas of the church respect the transcendence of the mystery while trying to praise and illumine it. It is interesting to note that the christological heresies, especially Arianism, which tended to reduce the mystery of God to rationalistic theory, were often favored by the state. Such formulations, because they failed adequately to grasp the radical transcendence of God and God's Word over all human institutions and systems, even mathematical systems, were easier to integrate into a rational political ideology and therefore were more useful to the state than orthodoxy, which preserved the freedom, transcendence and mystery of God. Unfortunately, ecclesiastical and secular politicians all too often were (and are) able to find ways of combining doctrinal orthodoxy with political heresy (idolatry) in order to legitimate the social and political status quo. I believe that liberation theology's emphasis on orthopraxis represents a challenge to overcome this contradiction between orthodox doctrine and heretical politics that has been too characteristic of the church since the Constantinian settlement.

5. Jürgen Moltmann, *The Trinity and the Kingdom* (New York: Harper & Row, 1981) 57. In this chapter I stress the positive aspects of the church's christological and trinitarian dogma, which expresses and contributes to much that is best and most unique in the Christian vision of God and understanding of the world. That reductionism that understands Christian faith as merely the acceptance of dogma, however, has done much harm to the faith. Christian faith is far more than dogma. Indeed, as Sobrino points out, "The intention behind dogma is not to exhaust the content of faith but to defend . . . some aspect

regarded as basic, against some error that threatens it" (*Christology at the Crossroads,* 317). Dogma, says Sobrino, is an explanation of Scripture and as such can never ignore or go beyond what is said in Scripture; in principle, it always says less than Scripture. In addition to these general limitations of dogma, Sobrino points out limitations of the christological and trinitarian dogmas of the early church, rooted in their dependence on the philosophical thinking of fourth- and fifth-century Hellenism. To Sobrino, these formulations "suffer from the lack of concreteness, historicity and relationality" (p. 329). Modern trinitarian and christological theologies, while incorporating the ontological affirmations of these ancient dogmas, need to focus on these dimensions of concreteness, historicity and relationality neglected in the historic formulations.

Grillmeyer supports Sobrino's analysis of the christological and trinitarian formulations of the early church. He writes, "These formulations clarify only one . . . point of belief in Christ. That in Jesus Christ, God really entered into human history and thus achieved our salvation. If the picture of Christ is to be illumined fully, these formulas must always be seen against the whole background of the biblical belief in Christ. . . . None of the formulas . . . should be given up. Yet not one of them can claim to be the Church's last word on a divine revelation" (*Christ in Christian Tradition,* 493).

6. Moltmann, *The Trinity and the Kingdom,* 57.

7. Ibid.

8. Moltmann, *The Trinity and the Kingdom,* xvi.

9. Ibid., 58.

10. Ibid., 59.

11. Gerard Manley Hopkins, *Poems and Prose* (Harmondsworth, Eng.: Penguin Books, 1953) 27.

12. For recent works on Christian faith and ecological responsibility, see Paul Santmire, *The Travail of Nature* (Philadelphia: Fortress Press, 1985); Dieter Hessel, *For Creation's Sake* (Philadelphia: Geneva Press, 1985). Hessel seeks to bring together the justice and ecology movements and uses the word "ecojustice" to express this relationship. The works of Joseph Sittler, a pioneer in the theology of creation, is one of the inspirations for these works, especially Santmire's. Matthew Fox's work to restore a creation-centered spirituality to Christianity is also relevant to this discussion.

13. Moltmann, *The Trinity and the Kingdom,* 23.

14. For Dietrich Bonhoeffer, the Christian knowledge of God as a suffering God is what distinguishes Christianity from religion. "Here is the decisive difference between Christianity and all religions. Man's religiosity makes him look in his distress to the power of God in the

world. God is the *deus ex machina*. The Bible directs man to God's powerlessness and suffering. Only the suffering God can help" (*Letters and Papers from Prison* [New York: Macmillan Co., 1972] 361).

15. I believe that too narrow an understanding of the work of the Spirit has prevailed in the Western church, where it is understood to be the nourishment and growth of the believer's inner life or the calling, gathering, sanctifying and enlightening of believers. Certainly these things are the work of the Spirit, but the Spirit also performs what might be called a more secular, worldly or cosmic function, the transfiguration of the whole created universe. This work is the context within which the transfiguration and sanctification of believers as well as the nourishing and renewing of the church should be understood. Moreover, believers are sanctified and the church renewed so that they can, in the power of the Spirit, participate in God's work of cosmic transfiguration. Cf. Moltmann, *The Trinity and the Kingdom*, 122–28; Alasdair Heron, *The Holy Spirit* (Philadelphia: Westminster Press, 1983) esp. chaps. 2–4.

16. Dietrich Bonhoeffer, *Ethics* (New York: Macmillan Co., 1955) 55.

17. Nicholas Berdyaev asserts, among other things, that "it is the Orthodox East which is closest to the idea of cosmic transfiguration and enlightenment" ("Salvation and Creativity: Two Understandings of Christianity," in *Western Spirituality: Historical Roots, Ecumenical Routes*, ed. Matthew Fox [Santa Fe, N.M.: Bear & Co., 1980] 128).

18. Georges Florovsky points out that the doctrine of the resurrection of the body was the most striking novelty in the original Christian message, at least in the Hellenistic world. He writes, "The Greek mind was rather disgusted by the body. . . . The Greeks dreamt of a complete and final *discarnation*. The expectation of a bodily resurrection would befit rather an earthworm, suggested Celsus, a second-century pagan philosopher who wrote against Christianity. To Celsus, this nonsense about a future resurrection seemed . . . altogether irreverent and irreligious. God would never do things so stupid, would never accomplish desires so criminal and capricious, which are inspired by an impure and fantastic love of the flesh" (*Creation and Redemption* [Springfield, Va.: Nordland, 1976] 111). Celsus calls Christians a *philosomatos genos* ("flesh-loving crew"). Florovsky notes that Christianity brought a new conception of the body into the ancient world. I believe this new conception of the body implies a new understanding of matter itself. Florovsky quotes John Chrysostom who, preaching on 2 Cor. 5:4, said that Paul "deals a death-blow here to those who deprecate the physical nature and revile our flesh. . . . It is not flesh . . . that we put off from ourselves, but corruption. The body is one thing, corruption is another. Nor is the body corruption, nor corruption the body. True, the

body is corrupt, but it is not corruption. . . . The body is the work of
God. . . . The future life shatters and abolishes not the body, but that
which clings to it, corruption and death" (*De resurrectione mortuorum,*
vol. 6, 427–28, quoted by Florovsky, p. 115).

Furthermore, Florovsky understands the resurrection of the body as
implying the transfiguration of the entire material universe. He writes,
"The resurrection is the true renewal, the transfiguration, the reforma-
tion of the whole creation" (p. 120). This transfiguration is not just a
return to an earlier, more perfect state such as that described in Genesis 1—3. Rather, through this transformation, the cosmos will be "for
the *first* time brought into that state, in which it ought to have been,
had not sin and the fall entered the world, but which was never
realized in the past" (p. 125).

19. Moltmann, *The Trinity and the Kingdom,* 124.

20. Dietrich Bonhoeffer, *The Cost of Discipleship* (New York, Macmillan Co., 1957) 60.

21. Thomas Parker, "The Political Meaning of the Trinity," *Journal of
Religion* 60, no. 2 (April 1980): 178.

22. Ibid., 179. For another detailed discussion of the political implications of the doctrine of the Trinity, see Moltmann, *The Trinity and the
Kingdom,* 191–201, 212–22.

23. Moltmann, *The Trinity and the Kingdom,* 57.

24. Ibid., 197.

25. Ibid. (emphasis mine).

26. G. A. Studdert Kennedy, *The Hardest Part* (London: Hodder &
Stoughton, 1925) 42.

ANNOTATED BIBLIOGRAPHY

CHAPTER 1.
SERPENTINE WISDOM IN AN AGE OF CRISIS

Sprout, Harold, and Margaret Sprout. *Toward a Politics for the Planet Earth.* New York: D. Van Nostrand, 1971.

This excellent book by Princeton international relations scholars and pioneers surveys the global political scene and enables us to see the world in some new ways. The Sprouts assert that all nations and peoples are interconnected with the environment and offer an impressive array of statistical and analytical facts to back up their assertion.

Teilhard de Chardin, Pierre. *The Phenomenon of Man.* New York: Harper & Brothers, 1959.

This visionary and poetic book by the Jesuit priest and paleontologist presents his personal interpretation of reality—an interpretation that is deeply influenced on the one hand by his vision of evolutionary development and on the other by his faith in a personal God revealed in Jesus of Nazareth. Teilhard de Chardin's work is a masterful and very influential effort to bring biblical faith and the modern evolutionary world view into fruitful relationship with each other.

Toffler, Alvin. *The Third Wave.* New York: Bantam Books, 1980.

This interesting study offers insights into the characteristics of our age. It supports many of the conclusions the Sprouts came to nine years earlier, showing how the intervening decade's developments tend to confirm their point of view.

CHAPTER 2.
THE DYNAMICS OF UNDERDEVELOPMENT

Chomsky, Noam, and Edward Herman. *The Washington Connection and Third World Fascism.* Boston: South End Press, 1979.

This book describes Pentagon and CIA involvements throughout the Third World from the 1950s through the 1970s. It documents extensive American involvements in military coups overthrowing democratically elected governments all over the world, as well as persistent American support for oppressive military dictatorships.

Lernoux, Penny. *The Cry of the People.* New York: Doubleday Co., 1980.

This book describes the misery of the Latin American people from the point of view of a Catholic journalist who has seen this misery close up. Lernoux emphasizes the role of the oligarchic elite, which has kept the people poor and powerless through intimidation, torture, execution and imprisonment.

ul Haq, Mabub. *The Poverty Curtain.* New York: Columbia University Press, 1976.

This book by a Pakistani economist and former World Bank vice-president criticizes past development processes and procedures, contrasts some myths of development with realities and offers some thoughts on a new international economic order.

CHAPTER 3.
THE NUCLEAR THREAT TO SURVIVAL

Aldridge, Robert. *The Counterforce Syndrome.* Washington, D.C.: The Center for Policy Studies, 1978.

This monograph is written by an aeronautical engineer who, before his religious conversion, worked for the engineering department of Lockheed and helped design every submarine-launched missile system purchased by the Navy. It describes in technical but understandable terms overall American strategic nuclear weapons and defense plans and concludes with an interesting comparison of American and Soviet strategic weapons systems. Though written in 1978, much of the information is still relevant.

Defense Monitor. Washington, D.C.: Center for Defense Information (monthly).

This periodical provides updates on defense-related issues, especially Soviet and American weapons systems. Staffed by former military personnel, it provides a strong critique of the military-industrial complex by people who have had experience within that complex.

North/South: A Program for Survival. Cambridge: MIT Press, 1980.

This report of the Brandt Commission to the United Nations describes the plight of the Third World and offers some suggestions for reform of the world economic system. It contains interesting chapters on the role of international financial institutions, transnational corporations, and international organizations and the relationship between development and disarmament.

CHAPTER 4.
GOD AND ISRAEL

Florovsky, George. *Creation and Redemption.* Springfield, Va.: Nordland Publishing Co., 1976.

This exciting book by a Russian Orthodox theologian articulates the cosmic and esthetic vision of Eastern Orthodoxy in a very appealing and stimulating way. Florovsky clearly shows that the split between matter and spirit, between creation and redemption, so characteristic of Western Christianity, is far less dominant in the Orthodox tradition. On the contrary, much Orthodox theology was developed consciously and explicitly to counter this split, which was considered a Platonist heresy.

Fox, Matthew. *Original Blessing.* Santa Fe, N.M.: Bear & Co., 1983.

In this book, Fox develops the biblical concept of original blessing as a balance to the Augustinian concept of original sin. Fox emphasizes the goodness of creation and attempts to bring justice and spirituality into an intimate relationship with each other.

Leach, Kenneth. *Experiencing God: Theology as Spirituality.* New York: Harper & Row, 1985.

This excellent book by a British theologian tracks the incarnational theme in Christian spirituality from its roots in the Bible through the period of the desert fathers to contemporary times. Its emphases are on the goodness of creation and the body and the relationship between Christian spirituality and justice. These emphases are developed through such themes as "God the Abyss," "God the Mother," and "God and Justice."

Lind, Millard C. *Yahweh Is a Warrior.* Scottdale, Pa.: Herald Press, 1980.

This study by a Mennonite biblical scholar presents a new and refreshing understanding of the Old Testament's picture of Yahweh as a warrior and of the associated Old Testament concept of Holy War. For people disturbed by the violence of the Old Testament's picture of God and eager to understand how such a God could be a peacemaker, Lind's book offers much that is of interest while maintaining respect for the texts themselves.

Miranda, José P. *Marx and the Bible.* Maryknoll, N.Y.: Orbis Books, 1974.

This book by a Mexican exegete builds a very persuasive case for understanding interhuman justice as the summary of God's will for the world. Amassing an impressive array of scholarly support, Miranda insists that the prophets, the law, Jesus and Paul all see justice as the service that God desires of all people.

Santmire, Paul. *The Travail of Nature.* Philadelphia: Fortress Press, 1985.

This is the best book I have found that relates Christian faith to the environment. It is informed by the Irenaean tradition, which, like Eastern Orthodoxy, understands creation, redemption and transfiguration as the one, ongoing work of the triune God. The chapter on St. Francis of Assisi is exceptional. Santmire was influenced by the pioneering work of Joseph Sittler in the area of Christianity and environment.

CHAPTER 5.
JESUS, GOD AND THE KINGDOM

Bonhoeffer, Dietrich. *Letters and Papers from Prison.* New York: Macmillan Co., 1953.

This book contains fragments written by Bonhoeffer after he was imprisoned for his participation in the July 1944 attempt to kill Hitler. These fragments contain Bonhoeffer's most creative thinking. It is in them that he develops his ideas about "religionless Christianity."

Jesudasan, Ignatius. *A Gandhian Theology of Liberation.* Maryknoll, N.Y.: Orbis Books, 1984.

This volume by an Indian Jesuit represents an original approach to Gandhi studies by a compatriot of Gandhi. It is a fascinating and stimulating study.

Jones, E. Stanley. *Gandhi, Portrayal of a Friend.* Nashville: Abingdon, 1983.

This beautiful biography by a Methodist missionary is both enlightening and inspirational. It is a must for anyone interested in Gandhi or Gandhian nonviolence.

Marx, Karl. *Writings of the Young Marx on Philosophy and Religion.* Edited by Lloyd Easton and Kurt Guddat. New York: Doubleday & Co., 1967.

This book contains some of the most important writings of the young Marx, written before *The Communist Manifesto.* It is especially important for an understanding of Marxist humanism and of the Marxist critique of religion.

Scott, Bernard Brandon. *Jesus, Symbol-Maker for the Kingdom.* Philadelphia: Fortress Press, 1981.

This well-written study of the parables is representative of a whole range of works that make use of literary criticism using some of the language and concepts of structuralism. This book helps us enter Jesus' world and understand Jesus' experience of God, which he sought to communicate through his parables. Scott emphasizes the unique nature of Jesus' parables and suggests that this uniqueness indicates how strongly the parables communicate Jesus' own personal vision of reality.

Segundo, Juan Luis. *The Historical Jesus of the Synoptics.* Maryknoll, N.Y.: Orbis Books, 1985.

The emphasis in this book by the Uruguayan theologian is on the conflict between Jesus and the religious and political establishment of first-century Palestine. The revolutionary nature of Jesus' life and teaching is brought out clearly and the opposition to Jesus on the part of the rulers is seen as a reaction to this nature.

Sharp, Gene. *Gandhi as a Political Strategist.* Boston: Porter Sargent, 1979.

This book, along with Sharp's *Social Power and Political Freedom* (Boston: Porter Sargent, 1980), is an extraordinarily insightful interpretation of Gandhi's contribution to politics. Sharp, probably the best American Gandhi interpreter, shows that Gandhian politics is based upon the presupposition that the power of rulers is based on the consent and cooperation of the ruled. Both of these books document the many successes of political strategies based on this presupposition. Of particular interest in *Social Power and Political Freedom* is the chapter describing a large number of successful nonviolent campaigns against the Nazis in World War II.

Theissen, Gerd. *The Sociology of Early Palestinian Christianity.* Philadelphia: Fortress Press, 1977.

This interesting book describes the life style adopted by many of the earlier followers of Jesus, who largely abandoned private property and traditional family relationships in favor of community and itinerant preaching. This life style was predicated on the urgency of spreading Jesus' message and depended largely on the hospitality of other members of the Jesus community who had not made so radical a break with conventional life.

CHAPTER 6.
THE POLITICAL SIGNIFICANCE OF JESUS'
DEATH AND RESURRECTION

Moltmann, Jürgen. *The Crucified God.* New York: Harper & Row, 1974.

This highly quoted and influential study by the German theologian stresses the relationship between Jesus' life and teaching and his death. Moltmann sees both a political and a religious significance in Jesus' crucifixion. The political significance is that Jesus, and particularly the crucifixion of Jesus, represented a challenge in the deepest sense to the Roman political system and its gods. The religious significance is that Jesus' crucifixion revealed new mysteries of God's love and led to a revolutionary understanding of God and of God's way of working in the world. This new understanding emphasizes not the immutability but the *passion* of God—thus the title *The Crucified God.*

Sobrino, Jon. *Christology at the Crossroads.* Maryknoll, N.Y.: Orbis Books, 1978.

This creative book by the Spanish Jesuit is very similar to Moltmann's, but reflects Sobrino's long experience with the poor in El Salvador and is thus more concrete. Sobrino's reflections on the resurrection and his chapter on the prayer of Jesus are particularly original and insightful.

CHAPTER 7.
THE PASCHAL MYSTERY AS REVELATION OF GOD

Bonhoeffer, Dietrich. *Ethics.* New York: Macmillan Co., 1955.

This book was never finished by Bonhoeffer but was put together by Eberhard Bethge after Bonhoeffer's execution. Bethge used the sections written by Bonhoeffer in Berlin 1940–1943. In these writings, Bonhoeffer attempts a fresh approach to Christian ethics that roots it in a Christian interpretation of reality. Bonhoeffer develops the categories of the "ultimate" and the "penultimate" and perhaps a new way of talking about the two kingdoms. The section on the "natural," in which Bonhoeffer tries to reclaim the natural for God and secure it against the dangers of the "unnatural," is very creative. The Nazi context within which Bonhoeffer wrote clearly influences his interpretation; he sought to build a Christian case against the desecration and brutalization of life by the Nazis.

Moltmann, Jürgen. *The Trinity and the Kingdom.* New York: Harper & Row, 1981.

This book, along with Moltmann's *God in Creation* (New York: Harper & Row, 1983), represents a further development in his theology. The christology of *The Crucified God* led to reflections on the doctrine of the Trinity, which are the subject matter of this book. Moltmann's ecumenical theology is extremely stimulating. Of particular interest are the influences of Eastern Orthodoxy on Moltmann. His understanding of the Trinity is more influenced by the sociological interpretation of Eastern Christianity than by the psychological interpretation of Augustine and is therefore especially intriguing to Western Christians.

SUBJECTS AND NAMES

acculturation, 24–26
Alamogordo, N.M., 49
Aldridge, R., 170
Allende, S., 47
American civil religion, 25
Anselm of Canterbury, 66–67, 151 n.2
Arevelo, J.J., 46
Armos, C.C., 46
Athanasius, 129

B-1 bomber, 52
Bainton, R., 160 n.53
baptism, 2, 131, 138
Barnet, R., 18, 145 n.16
Barry, T., 147 nn.10–13
Barth, K., 66–67, 151 n.2
Bartsch, H.W., 146 n.35
basic Christian communities, 45
Berdyaev, N., 135, 137, 155 n.31, 166
    n.17
Bergraav, E., 141
Bergson, H., 28, 144 n.4, 146 n.37
Biot, F., 71, 153 n.13
Bondurant, J., 160 n.52
Bonhoeffer, D., 135, 139, 144 n.8, 152
    n.5, 156 n.1, 161 n.60, 165 n.14, 166
    n.16, 167 n.20, 172, 174
Bosch, J., 47
Brandt, W., 144 n.3
Brazil, 47
Breech, J., 157, n.11
Brueggemann, W., 70, 83, 153 nn.10–11;
    154 n.29

Brown, L., 38
Buber, M., 134
Bultmann, R., 26–27, 107, 146 n.35, 160
    n.39, 161 n.5

Cabot, J.M., 46
Cadoux, C.F., 160 n.53
Camara, Dom Helder, 42, 141, 148 n.21
Cappadocians, 129
Cardonnal, J., 71, 153 n.12
Carter, J., 52
Cassidy, R., 112, 161 n.56
Celsus, 166 n.18
Cervantes, M. de, 22
Chalcedon, 130
Chatfield, C., 144 n.3
Chavez, C., 148 n.21
Chernobyl, 146 n.30
Childs, B., 154 n.23
Chile, 47
China, 38
Chomsky, N., 148, n.20, 149 n.30, 170
Chrysostom, John, 109, 159 n.26, 166
    n.18, 167 n.18; liturgy of, 154 n.26
CIA, 47
Cobb, J., 27
cold war, ending of, 21
Conroy, M., 151 n.3
Constantine, 128
cosmos, 88–90, 132-34; consummation of,
    90; and ecumenical dialogue, 88; and
    gnosticism, 88; goodness of, 89;
    groaning of, 90; and incarnation, 90;

and justice, 134, 155 n.34, 156 n.34;
and love of God, 132; mending of, 90;
and peace, 133; and redemption, 88;
and sacrament of God, 89; and shalom,
90; stewardship of, 89, 133; and torah,
90; and Trinity, 132; and wisdom
literature, 88
Croser, L., 146
Crossan, J.D., 94, 96–97, 100, 157 n.11,
158 n.22
cruise missile, 52–53
Cullmann, O., 162 n.10

Davey, C., 151 n.1
Davidowitz, L., 145 n.15
Day, D., 141, 148 n.21
deBeauvoir, S., 14, 145 n.12
Dimas, L.J., 55
Dobyns, H., 144 n.10
Dominican Republic, 47
Douglas, J., 159 n.38
Dulles, A., 46
Dulles, J.F., 46

Easton, L.D., 154 n.22, 156 n.2, 161 n.2
Ebeling, G., 158 n.18
ecojustice, 165
Ehrlich, A. and P., 38, 155 n.33
Einstein, A., 49, 60, 151 n.32
Elliot, T.S., 59
Energy, Department of, 52
Englander, H., 70, 152 n.7, 153 n.8–9
Engels, F., 146 n.36, 154 n.22
Enuma Elish, 89
environment, 22–24
Erikson, E., 159 n.33, 160 n.51
eucharist, 2, 128, 131, 138
evolution, 60
exodus, 70–75; as archetype, 72; and
liberation, 71–72; as revelation of God,
70; and slavery, 70; and torah, 72–73
Ezra, 68

Falwell, J., 146 n.34
Faulkner, W., 59
First World, 31, 38, 40
Florovsky, G., 155 n.31, 166 n.18, 171
Folk, J., 151 n.20, 160 n.53
Ford, J.M., 159 n.38
Forest, J., 151 n.23
Fourth World, 31
Fox, M., 130, 151 n.4, 155 nn.31–32, 34
Francis of Assisi, 172
French, M., 145 n.16
Fretheim, T., 80, 134, 154 n.24
Friere, P., 44, 144 n.9, 149 n.27
Frierro, A., 71–72
Fromm, E., 112, 161 n.55
Fulton, R., 149 n.1

Galtung, J., 47–48, 149 n.33
Gandhi, M.K., 13, 109–10, 141, 148 n.18,
152 n.4, 159 n.33, 160 nn.50–52
Geiger, J., 150 n.12
Genovese, E.D., 144 n.11
Gilbert, M., 145 n.15
Gold, D., 56, 151 n.19
Gorbachev, M., 145 n.22
Gottwald, N.K., 153 nn.13–14
Goulart, J., 47
Grace, W.R., 46
Gray, E.D., 146 n.32
Gremillion, J., 149 n.26
Griffin, D.R., 27
Grillmeyer, A., 156 n.35, 162 n.1, 164
n.4, 165 n.5
Guddat, K., 154 n.22
Guatemala, 36, 45–46
Guolet, D., 159 n.26
Guzman, J.A., 46

Heering, G.J., 160 n.53
Heidegger, M., 26
Herman, E., 148 n.20, 149 n.28
Herod Antipas, 111
Heron, A., 166 n.15
hesed, 81
Heschel, A., 134
Hessel, D., 146 n.32
Hilberg, R., 145 n.15
Hildegard of Bingen, 155–56 n.34
Hiroshima, 50–53, 58, 149 n.2, 150 n.9
Hitler, A., 46
holocaust, 15
Hopkins, G.M., 133, 165 n.11
Hussein, S., 15
Huxley, A., 32

Ignatius of Antioch, 123
International Monetary Fund, 43
Iraq, 21
Irenaeus of Lyon, 114, 123, 128, 140, 154
n.26, 155 n.32, 156 n.35
ITT, 47

Jantzen, G., 155 n.33
Jeremias, J., 100
Jesudassan, I., 172
Jesus, 4, 29, 67, 91–131, 134–37, 156 n.3;
and the Kingdom of God, 93–101; and
love of enemies, 106–13; and
nationalism, 110–13; parables of,
93–100; and the poor, 102–4; and
sinners, 113–16
Joanna, 106
John Paul II, 15, 143 n.2
Jones, E.S., 109, 160 n.52, 173
jubilee year, 74, 101
Jung, C.G., 157 n.8
Justin Martyr, 122

Käsemann, E., 93, 157 n.7
Kennecott Copper, 47
Kennedy, S., 140
Kingdom of God, 11, 93–108, 115–18, 128
King, M.L., Jr., 13, 110, 141, 152 n.4
Kittel, G., 143 n.1
Klassen, W., 107–8, 159 n.38, 160 nn.39–41
Ku Klux Klan, 15
Kuwait, 21

laissez faire, 75
Land, P., 43, 148 n.24
Lash, C., 59, 151 n.26
latifundia, 39
Leach, K., 171
Lenz, T., 145 n.24
Lernoux, P., 15, 145 n.14
less developed countries (LDC), 37–38, 41–43
Lessing, G.E., 157 n.5
Lifton, R., 59, 151 n.26
Limburg, J., 155 n.33
Lind, M., 77–78, 153 nn.19–21
Lodge, H.C., 46
logos, 129, 130
Lutz, C.P., 151 n.20, 160 n.53

McFague, S., 146 n.32
McHarg, I., 155 n.33
MacGregor, G.H.C., 109, 161 n.53
Mandelbaum, M., 59, 151 n.25
Marduk, 89
Martha of Bethany, 106
Mary Magdalene, 106
Marx, K., 9, 24, 91, 119, 146 n.31, 144 n.7, 146 n.31, 154 n.22, 156 n.2
Marxism, 9, 11, 144 n.7
Mary of Bethany, 106
Medellin, 44
Melman, S., 55–56, 150 nn.16–18
Merton, R.K., 22, 146 n.28
microfundia, 39
Middle East, 49
minifundia, 39
Minuteman III missiles, 51–52
Miranda, J.P., 11, 144 n.7, 146 n.36, 153 nn.16, 18; 154 n.22, 158 n.13, 172
Moltmann, J., 11, 119–21, 124–25, 131–32, 134, 144 n.6, 161 nn.5–8; 162 nn.9, 11, 15, 24, 26; 164 n.5, 165 nn.6–10, 13; 166 n.15, 167 nn.19, 23–25; 174–75
Morris, M., 58
MX missile, 52

Nagasaki, 50–53, 149–50 n.9
Nahum, 68
Nelson, J.B., 145 n.13
new creation, 3

New International Order, 42
new world order, 21
Newcomb, T., 146
Newtonian, 26
Nicea, 130
Niebuhr, R., 109, 160 nn.43–44

O'Collins, G., 162 n.15
Origen, 129
Owensby, W., 147

Pallmeyer, J.N., 45, 149 n.29
Pannenberg, W., 123–24, 162 nn.16–19
Parker, T., 167 nn.21–22
Parsons, T., 146
Paul the Apostle, 135–36
Paul VI, 36–37, 44, 57, 143 n.2, 147 n.15, 148 n.17, 149 n.25, 151 n.21
Perrin N., 94, 96, 157 n.10, 158 n.15
Persian Gulf, 21, 49
Pilate, 120
Pinochet, A., 47
Pittenger, N., 27
Platt, J., 49
Preusch, D., 147 nn.8–10
powers and principalities, 2–3
Poseidon missile, 51–52

Quixote, Don, 21

Rasmussen, L., 157 n.4
Reagan, R., 52
Reimarus, H.S., 92, 157 n.5
Rich, A., 145 n.16
Robertson, P., 146 n.34
Robinson, J.M., 157 n.4
Rostow, W.W., 35
Rougemont, D., 19
Rublev, A., 132
Ruth, 68

Sabbath, B., 147 n.4
sacraments, 2, 131
Sadako, 50, 149
salvation, 2
Sanders, E.P., 100, 158 n.22, 159 n.23
Santmire, P., 155 nn.32, 34; 156 n.35, 165 n.17
Schell, J., 50, 149 n.4
Schnackenberg, R., 162 n.15
Schneidman, E.S., 58–59, 149 n.1, 151 nn.24, 29–30
Schottroff, L., 109, 160 n.47
Schweitzer, A., 92, 157 n.6
Schweitzer, E., 107, 160 n.41
Second Isaiah, 68
Second World, 31
Segundo, J.L., 100–101, 109, 113–15, 159 n.28, 160 n.46, 161 nn.57–59, 61; 162 nn.15, 21; 173
shalom, 2, 68, 84–85, 138

Shange, N., 145 n.16
Sharp, G., 160 n.52, 173
Shils, E., 141
Sider, R., 150 n.10, 152 n.6
Sittler, J., 155 n.32, 165 n.12
Smith, W.B., 46
Sobrino, J., 121–22, 124–25, 162
    nn.12–14, 20, 25–27; 163 n.4, 165 n.5,
    174
Soviet Union, 31, 49, 51–52, 54, 57–58,
    110, 136, 145 n.14
Spretnak, C., 163 n.3
Sprout, H. and M., 16, 21, 24, 131, 143
    n.3, 145 nn.17, 25–27; 169
Star Wars, 21
Starhawk, 163 n.3
State Department, 47
Stendahl, K., 90
Suzanna, 106
Swidler, L., 108–9, 159 nn.30–37

Tanzania, 38
Taylor, J., 147
Taylor, R., 160 n.48
Teilhard de Chardin, Pierre, 10, 28, 144
    n.4, 152 n.4, 169
Temple, W., 2
Teresa, Mother, 148 n.21
Tertullian, 136
Theissen, G., 10, 28, 103, 144 n.4, 152
    n.4, 159 nn.25–26; 174
Third World, 31, 35–36, 38–44, 48,
    146–47 nn.1, 16

Thistlethwaite, S., 163 n.2
Tiamat, 89
Tiberius Caesar, 111
Todaro, M.P., 31, 36–38, 147 nn.2–3, 14;
    148 nn.18–19, 41
Torah, 72–75
Trident: submarine, 52; Trident I missile,
    52; Trident II missile, 52
Trinity, 127–41, 163–67, 175
Trinity test site, 49
Trocmé A., 158 n.24
Tsipis, K., 54, 150 n.14
Tugwell, R.G., 151 n.28
Tutu, D., 141

ul Haq, M., 148 n.23
United States Marines, 47
Ubico, J., 46
Union of Concerned Scientists, 21
United Church of Christ, 58
United Fruit Company, 45–47
United Nations, 21, 40, 42, 57, 148 n.22

van Ruysbroek, J., 67, 151 n.3
von Rad, G., 81, 153 n.16, 154 n.27

Walker, A., 145 n.16
Wingren, G., 155 n.32

Yoder, J.H., 158 n.24, 159 n.28

zealot, 120

SCRIPTURE

OLD TESTAMENT

Genesis
1—3—167
2:7–9, 15, 18—89

Exodus
1—15—79
12:17–20—98
20:2–4, 7—72
20:22–23—73
21:23–25—27
22:25—74
23:22—73

Leviticus
17—26—73
19:9–10—73
23:22—73
25:8–55—74
25:36–37—74

Deuteronomy
10:18–19—74
15:1–18—73
23:19–20—74
24:19–21—73

Psalms
30:5—80
85:3—80
85:10—85

Proverbs
29:18—8

Isaiah
2:1–4—85–86
9:5–6—85
11:6–9—84
31:1—83
49:6—87
53:5–6—87
54:7–8—80

Ezekiel
17:23—98

Hosea
11:1–3—80
11:8–9—86

Amos
5:21–24—103
6:6—83

NEW TESTAMENT

Matthew
5:38–48—107
5:39—109
8:20—103
10:16—4
12:22–32—115
13:31–32—98, 104

15:2—114
21:31—114
25—2
25:31–46—34, 115
26:52—108
26:55–56—112

Mark
2:27—114
4:30–32—98
5:25–34—105
8:33b—108
9:35—118
10:17–22—103
10:23–24—103
12:14–17—111
14:47—108
14:48–49—112

Luke
6:20–23—102
6:24–26—102
6:27–37—107
7:36–50—115
8:1–3—106
8:8—99
8:43–48—105
10:38–42—104
11:27–28—104
13:10–17—114
13:18–19—98
13:20–21—98, 105
13:31–32—111

13:34—105
14:23—99
15:3–32—104
16:1–19—4
16:19–31—103
18:9–14—114
18:17—118
18:22–23—112
20:22–25—111
22:24–26—111
22:52–53—112
23:34—108
23:49–51—108

John
7:37–39—105

8:3–11—115
8:7—115
9:1–12—114
18:10–11—108

Romans
8:18–25—138
8:21–24—90
10:11—110

1 Corinthians
1:18–25—135

2 Corinthians
5:4—166

Galatians
3:29—110

Ephesians
1:10—90
2:11–22—110

Colossians
1:5–23—110
1:15–20—110
1:19–29—116
3:11—110

1 John
4:6—80, 131